BATH
HISTORY

BATH HISTORY

VOLUME VI

edited by Brenda J. Buchanan

Millstream Books
1996

Bath History gratefully acknowledges the support of the following organisations:

Bath & North East Somerset Heritage Services
Bath Archaeological Trust
Bath Preservation Trust
The Bath Society
The History of Bath Research Group
Advanced Studies in England

First published 1996 by
Millstream Books, 18 The Tyning, Bath BA2 6AL

ISBN 0 948975 42 3

Set in 10 on 12 point Palatino and printed by
Antony Rowe Ltd, Bumper's Farm, Chippenham SN14 6LH

CONTENTS

In the Notes at the end of each article in this volume, the place of publication of books is London unless otherwise stated.

NOTES ON CONTRIBUTORS

Robert Bell M.A. has been a professional archaeologist for over twenty years. Since 1984 he has worked for Bath Archaeological Trust, directing excavations at a wide variety of different sites ranging from prehistoric settlements to eighteenth-century gardens, both within Bath and elsewhere in the West of England.

Nicholas von Behr has worked as a museum researcher in industrial history in Bristol and Bath. After a first degree at the University of Bristol he completed an M.Sc. in Social Research at the University of Bath in 1995. His main work was on the emergence of factory manufacture in the Twerton cloth industry.

J.H.Bettey was Reader in Local History at the University of Bristol, from where he holds a Ph.D. He is the author of numerous books and articles on west-country history, especially on the agriculture, rural society, churches and church life of Bristol, Somerset, Dorset and Wiltshire. Recent publications include *Estates in the English Countryside* (1993) and *Man and the Land: Farming in Dorset 1846-1996* (1996).

Brenda Buchanan is a Visiting Fellow at the University of Bath. She holds a Ph.D. of the University of London for her research on investment in North Somerset in the eighteenth century, and has contributed articles to several journals on this theme. She was the first Chairman of the History of Bath Research Group, from 1986 to 1991.

A.J.Keevil has since his retirement developed his interest in local history. He has undertaken research into some of its less well-known aspects, such as the route of the Fosseway through the Bath area, published in the *Proceedings of the Somerset Archaeological & Natural History Society* and the *Newsletter* of The Bath Survey Group.

Helena Lim is a researcher at the University of Bath, preparing her doctoral thesis on the premium system operated by agricultural societies such as the Bath & West Society and the Society of Arts in London. Her wider interests include innovation and technological transfer, particularly during the Agricultural Revolution.

Susan Sloman is Keeper of Collections at the Victoria Art Gallery, Bath. She has written extensively on British art in the eighteenth century, concentrating latterly on Thomas Gainsborough in Bath. She is currently writing a thesis on this subject as a research student at the University of Bristol.

Alex Kolaczkowski is a history teacher of wide experience in secondary schools. In 1995 she was awarded a doctorate by the University of Bath for her research on local government in the nineteenth century, with Bath as a case study. She is Secretary of the Bath Branch of the Historical Association and on the Committee of the History of Bath Research Group.

BATH ABBEY: SOME NEW PERSPECTIVES

Robert Bell

Bath Abbey has been the subject of detailed historical study in recent years. In particular, the archaeological and architectural evidence has been discussed by Peter Davenport in an earlier volume of *Bath History*,[1] while Jean Manco has written a detailed account of the documentary sources.[2] However a further article can be justified because, in the short time since their publication, a significant amount of new archaeological evidence relating to the lay-out of the Saxon abbey precinct and of the Norman cathedral priory has been recovered. Of particular value were the excavations carried out by Bath Archaeological Trust during 1993 in advance of the construction of the Abbey Heritage Centre (immediately south of the Abbey), and also beneath York Street in 1994-5.

The earliest documentary reference to a monastic house at Bath is in a charter issued in 676 by Osric, King of the Hwicce, granting 100 hides of land to Abbess Berta to found a convent. But Christians were known in Bath back in the third century, judging by the inscription on one of the lead curses retrieved from the King's Bath spring in 1979, and any study of the origins of Christian worship in Bath should begin in the late-Roman rather than the Saxon period.

The late-Roman and sub-Roman period

Aquae Sulis was very far from being a typical Roman small town. The area occupied by the medieval walled city was, in Roman times, one of the most important pagan cult centres in Britain, serving as both a religious sanctuary and a health spa. It was dominated by the Temple of Sulis Minerva and the Baths, which were constructed around the Sacred Spring from the second half of the first century onwards, almost certainly replacing an earlier Celtic shrine. The sanctuary, enclosed in the mid to late second century by a ditch and rampart, was extensive and appears to have contained several subsidiary shrines, including one at the Cross Bath and one at the Hot Bath (where there was also another, smaller baths complex). In addition, a circular shrine or *tholos* is thought to have been located on the vaulted podium to the east of the precinct of the Temple of Minerva.

The nucleus of the actual town was, however, at Walcot, c.1km north of the Sacred Spring. The most likely explanation for its location is that it originated as a civilian market or *vicus*, serving a mid-first century military fort protecting the main river crossing in the vicinity of Cleveland Bridge. The settlement rapidly developed alongside the approach roads, extending southwards towards the sanctuary.

In the early fourth century, the sanctuary was still flourishing. For example, the inner precinct of the Temple of Minerva was repaved and the steps leading up to the temple were re-treaded. Elsewhere an open-ended building, discovered in 1993, was constructed in the late third century on a former open space immediately east of the Baths. It seems to have been a shop selling pewter vessels. These were manufactured in the workshop at the rear, where two stone moulds were found, and may have been aimed specifically at the pilgrim market. The most dramatic evidence for the continuing prosperity of the cult centre is the circuit wall, inserted in front of the second-century rampart and enclosing the whole of the sanctuary. It was probably also built at this time, and although it was subsequently utilized as the Saxon and medieval town wall, in origin it may have been designed to protect only the religious complex. The civilian town outside remained undefended.

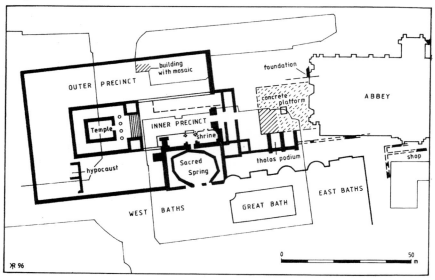

1. Plan of the Temple of Sulis Minerva and its precinct in the mid to late fourth century. To the east are the foundations of a vaulted podium, replaced by a concrete platform on which the earliest church may have stood. *(Drawing by Kirsty Rodwell)*

By the mid-fourth century, however, the sanctuary was being transformed (fig. 1). The colonnade round the outer precinct of the Temple of
Minerva was demolished and the inner precinct was in decay. The number
of coins thrown into the Sacred Spring shows a marked decline from the
mid-350s onwards.[3] However the sanctuary was certainly not abandoned,
and a number of new buildings of this period, some of which were clearly
of high quality and contained mosaics and hypocausts, have been found.
A large building was erected outside the west wall of the outer precinct
and two others actually encroached on the precinct itself.[4]

  A possible explanation for these changes is that after the adoption of
Christianity as the official religion of the Roman Empire pagan worship
declined. The former sanctuary was secularized as the extra-mural town
migrated to a more defensible location. According to this theory *Aquae
Sulis* followed the pattern of other small late-Roman towns such as *Cunetio*
(Mildenhall, Wilts), which also acquired defensive walls. It should be said
that there are no clear signs that the extra-mural settlement actually was
abandoned in the fourth century. On the contrary, excavations on the *Hat
and Feather* site at Walcot in 1991-2 indicated that the buildings there
continued in use till the end of the fourth century, if not beyond. But it is
possible that the villa-owning aristocracy were looking to the former
religious complex as a safe haven in the troubled times of the second half
of the fourth century.

There is no unequivocal evidence that the pagan sanctuary was
Christianized in the late-Roman period. Some of the changes at *Aquae
Sulis* follow a pattern noted at other temple complexes in the region, where
ancillary buildings fell into decay and were demolished while the temple
itself was subdivided into smaller compartments.[5] The outer precinct of
the Temple of Minerva may have ceased to have a religious function but
parts of the inner precinct remained in use. In the late fourth century a
small area of the south portico, adjacent to the opening on the north side
of the Sacred Spring, was walled off, possibly to form a shrine. This is as
likely to have been pagan as Christian.

Evidence for the survival of Christian worship in the West Country in
the fifth century derives mainly from cemeteries. At Shepton Mallet, for
example, a fifth-century silver amulet cross with a punched Chi-Rho
symbol was discovered in 1990 in a burial associated with the settlement
alongside the Fosse Way,[6] while mausolea in the cemetery at Poundbury,
outside the Roman city of Dorchester, Dorset, are thought to be Christian.[7]
Bath's extra-mural cemeteries may also contain Christian artefacts and
structures, and it has been suggested that the present church of St Swithin,

Walcot, and the old church of St John, Bathwick, close to known cemeteries, may both owe their origins to sub-Roman mausolea.[8]

But it is clear that religious activity also continued in the centre of the walled area. Excavations beneath the Pump Room between 1981 and 1983 revealed a sequence of six cobbled surfaces separated by layers of soil which had accumulated above the paved floor of the inner precinct. The earliest of these surfaces must have been laid after the mid-fourth century, perhaps after 400. The latest is most unlikely to have gone out of use before the late fifth century and could conceivably be sixth- or even seventh-century in date. The latest surface incorporated a sculptured stone from the pediment of the temple (and may also have utilized the other parts of the pediment, including the Gorgon's head, which were recovered in the 1790s). It was not simply a piece of fallen rubble; it had been carefully laid upside down as paving. All the surfaces were heavily worn, especially in the vicinity of the opening to the Sacred Spring, which was clearly still being visited on a regular basis.[9]

There are striking similarities with the excavated Temple of Mercury at Uley in Gloucestershire, where the pagan temple, after modification in the late fourth century, was demolished in the early fifth century. In the mid-late fifth century, a hall or basilican church with a stone baptistery annexe was constructed on the site, and in turn this was replaced by an early sixth-century stone structure, thought to be a church. The floors of the fifth-century baptistery included re-used pagan altars, also laid upside down, and the head of the cult statue of Mercury was buried adjacent to the church.[10] It has been suggested that the pagan temple site was ritually cleansed before becoming Christianized, and the same explanation could apply at Bath, particularly given the existence of the bronze head of the cult statue of Minerva, discovered beneath Stall Street in 1727.

At Bath, no Christian structures have been identified in the precinct, but they may have been located near by, perhaps standing on the podium of the main temple. An alternative, and more plausible, location might be the massive concrete and rubble platform to the east of the precinct, recorded beneath the west end of the present Abbey by James Irvine in 1868. Another part of the same structure was briefly observed and then destroyed during the construction of the Pump Room extension in 1893.[11] The date and function of this structure is unclear but it seems to have replaced the second-century vaulted podium on which the *tholos* may originally have stood. The south wall of the podium, part of which is still visible within the Roman Baths Museum, was evidently partially rebuilt either at the very end of the Roman period or in the post- Roman period.

Following the analogy of Uley, it is also possible that the Sacred Spring was utilized as a baptistery.

Bath had clearly ceased to function as a town during the early fifth century, and the city of Bath, ruled by a king, which was captured by the West Saxons after the Battle of Dyrham in 577, is thought to have been an extensive estate rather than a city in the Roman sense. The centre of administration was probably outside the former town and one possible location which has been proposed is Little Solsbury hillfort.[12] However the religious centre of the estate is likely to have remained in the middle of Bath, focussed on the Sacred Spring. Interestingly, the habit of 'taking the waters' seems to have been popular, judging by the fragments of glass cups found in the layers of soil between the accumulating cobble layers. The survival of Christianity through the so-called 'Dark Ages' need not come as any surprise, although the traditional historical interpretation is that the walled area of Bath was completely abandoned during this period. Common sense suggests that a natural phenomenon as unusual as the hot spring, with its medicinal powers and its centuries-old tradition as a focus of religious worship, was surely not going to be neglected for 250 years, and the archaeological evidence supports this view. In contrast to the eastern and southern parts of the country, which fell under pagan Saxon rule at a fairly early stage, the West Country remained under British control for much longer, and there is no reason why Christianity should not have survived. Numerous places in south-east Wales and the Wye Valley acquired monasteries and ecclesiae in the late sixth and early seventh centuries,[13] and continuity of Christian worship at Bath ought perhaps to be seen as the norm in this region rather than as anything exceptional.

The Saxon Abbey

With this background the establishment of a Saxon religious house at Bath should therefore not necessarily be seen as a dramatic innovation. To summarize the limited documented evidence, a nunnery was founded by King Osric of the Hwicce in 676. There is no further mention of it after the seventh century and in c.758 a Mercian land charter refers to the brethren of St Peter's monastery. It is unclear whether this monastery was the direct descendant of Osric's convent, as the medieval monks evidently believed, or a completely new foundation. In 781 King Offa of Mercia claimed Bath Abbey from the Bishop of Worcester, by which time it was, according to the charter, 'celebrated'. The sources are silent throughout the ninth century but in the early tenth century Bath came under the political control of Wessex, and the monastery benefited considerably from royal patronage. In the 930s King Athelstan made substantial land-grants and further grants were made by King Edwy in 956 (when the hot springs were mentioned), and 957, when the Abbey was described as 'marvellously wrought'. After King Edgar came to the throne in 959, the monastery was reformed by Dunstan, Archbishop of Canterbury and former Abbot of Glastonbury, and brought under Benedictine rule. In 973 Bath Abbey enjoyed its greatest moment when it was the scene of Edgar's coronation as King of England by Dunstan.[14]

The precise location of the Saxon monastery is unknown. It has been the subject of considerable speculation and some writers have suggested that it was nowhere near the present Abbey. In the nineteenth century James Irvine suggested it might be near the Hot Bath spring in the south-west quarter of the City, while more recently Elizabeth Holland and Mike Chapman have proposed a site west of Stall Street, just to the south of Westgate Street.[15] The problem will only be solved by archaeological excavation, though this method is hampered by the virtual absence of coins and other datable artefacts in Bath between the fifth and early tenth centuries. An early eighth-century Danish coin was found at Mill Lane, Bathampton in 1994 during the construction of the Batheaston by-pass, but nothing comparable has been recovered from the centre of Bath. Similarly there is no recognizable pottery earlier than c.930 apart from two sherds of chaff-tempered ware from Swallow Street which can be dated to any time between 400 and 900.[16] Part of a fifth- to seventh-century brooch and a seventh- to eighth-century loom-weight were recovered from the Bath Street site in 1986, but with the exception of these objects, there are no Saxon artefacts earlier than the tenth century. An obvious conclusion to draw from this lack of material would be that the seventh-century nunnery and Offa's monastery were located outside the walled area of Bath. But this may well be incorrect. The absence of middle-Saxon pottery is not unique to Bath. The whole of Gloucestershire and Somerset appears to have been aceramic for 500 years, and excavations at the Saxon Cathedral at Wells produced no Saxon pottery at all.[17] The only other available dating method is radio-carbon analysis and this is very far from precise. As a result it is very difficult to demonstrate the presence of middle-Saxon features unless they are cut through known late-Roman deposits and are sealed by late-Saxon horizons. In the absence of any artefacts other then residual Roman material, it is perfectly possible that middle-Saxon walls have been mistakenly identified as late-Roman.

There is marginally more diagnostic late-Saxon material, though pottery from this period is still relatively uncommon and is only found in fairly small quantities. Although Bath was a defensible *burgh* from King Alfred's reign onwards and by the early tenth century was re-emerging as a town with its own mint, late-Saxon coins are still a rarity. The most easily recognisable artefacts of tenth- to eleventh-century date are sculptured stones, usually cross fragments.

The general lack of dating evidence provides one explanation for the failure to find the Saxon abbey. A second explanation is that several potential locations are either inaccessible to archaeologists or were destroyed, with little or no record, in the Georgian and Victorian periods. An obvious place to look is beneath the floor of the Norman cathedral nave, but this is c.2m below the level of the present church floor. It was raised in the early sixteenth century and most of the space between the two floors was subsequently filled with post-medieval burial vaults. It is almost impossible to reach the Norman floor, and even James Irvine, the clerk of works during the restoration of the Abbey in the 1860s, was unable to investigate beneath it. In other parts of the centre of Bath the post-Roman levels have been completely removed. The horizons above the East Baths, the Great and West Baths, and beneath the Concert Hall adjacent to the Pump Room ('excavated' in 1755, 1880-86 and 1893 respectively) might all have provided valuable evidence relating to the Saxon abbey, which has now been lost.

Nevertheless, despite these serious limitations, a certain amount of evidence has survived. Information about the earliest Saxon monastic house is negligible, but the tumble of very large Roman monumental stone blocks overlying the latest cobbled surface in the inner precinct may be of relevance. It is clear that the façade of the Four Seasons, along the south side of the precinct, and the entablature of the north wall of the Sacred Spring reservoir were intentionally demolished, perhaps in the late sixth or early seventh centuries, though possibly slightly later. They did not collapse of their own accord, and the purpose of the operation may have been to gain access to the smaller, more readily-usable coursed stones in the standing walls.[18] The only buildings likely to have been constructed of stone in this period were churches, and it is not inconceivable that the walls were dismantled by the builders of the monastery. Our view of Saxon Bath is heavily influenced by *The Ruin*, an evocative eighth-century poem which describes a landscape dominated by crumbling and abandoned buildings 'raised by giants'. To the poet they were an awesome sight. To the craftsmen working at the Abbey, they offered a readily-available quarry, and the footings of the only wall to have been found which is definitely Saxon consisted entirely of re-used Roman blocks.

This was discovered running east-west underneath York Street and had such massive foundations, 2.5m wide and at least 1.2m deep, that it has been interpreted as the free-standing south boundary wall of the monastic enclosure rather than part of a building. It cut through the east end wall of the East Baths, but pre-dated a late-Saxon burial. It could have been constructed before the tenth century, but it was certainly no later. Only a fairly short stretch of the wall has been revealed but it appears to be heading eastwards towards the Roman circuit wall, which probably served as the east wall of the precinct. The position of the north and west boundaries of the precinct are unknown. However a possible hypothesis is that the north wall ran parallel to the south side of Cheap Street (and was retained when the much larger Norman precinct was laid out at the end of the eleventh century), while the west wall utilized the surviving Roman wall dividing the Great Bath from the East Baths. The precinct wall would have served the same function as the large ditch and bank

2. Part of a row of graves in the late-Saxon cemetery to the south of the Abbey, above, from the east. *(Photograph by Bath Archaeological Trust)*

enclosing the Saxon abbey at Glastonbury.[19] One point of interest arising from its discovery is that the plan of the late-Saxon *burgh* needs to be reconsidered. As in other contemporary towns, Bath's road system was laid out in the form of a grid, which still survives in the northern half of the town. An earlier reconstruction of the lay-out suggested that High Street continued across the south half of the town beyond its junction with Cheap Street,[20] but the position of the precinct wall demonstrates that this southern extension cannot have existed. It remains unclear whether the enclosure was laid out in the tenth century, at the same time as the town, or whether, like the abbey church, it was already in existence and was respected by the road grid.

Within the precinct was a late-Saxon cemetery, which must surely be related to the monastery. It was first noted in 1755 when a mid-tenth-century coin-hoard was found in a grave. In 1968 Barry Cunliffe excavated a characteristically late-Saxon charcoal burial close to the north-east corner of the East Baths. But in 1993, a much larger area of the cemetery was recorded. The graves were laid out in regular rows, at right angles to the alignment of the present church (fig. 2). They would have been marked at ground level since each burial was distinct from its neighbour and there was no intercutting. Part of a decorated stone grave-cover and a marker-stone, re-used in a twelfth-century cist burial, must have been associated with these burials (fig. 3). The western and eastern limits of the cemetery are unknown, but it certainly extended from the second bay of the nave of the present Abbey as far as the second bay of the choir. It also extended southwards as far as the precinct wall. Thirty-one Saxon graves were found and the burials in eighteen of these were excavated. All the skeletons were adult and the great majority of those which were identifiable were male. Ten skeletons were buried in wooden coffins and eight were laid on a bed of charcoal. In six of the graves the skull was held upright with stones. A charnel pit, only part of which was excavated, contained the remains of at least thirty-three adults, which were disturbed and re-buried during the construction of the Norman cathedral. The date of the cemetery is provided by the coin-hoard, the grave-cover (thought to be late tenth-century) and three radio-carbon dates from charcoal burials, which all produced ninth- to tenth-century dates. It is worth noting that this was not the only late-Saxon cemetery in the vicinity. Burials of the same period, found beneath the Pump Room and Abbey Churchyard, are thought to have been associated with St Mary de Stalls Church, while another large cemetery, beneath Abbey Street and Abbey Green, is probably linked to St James's Church.

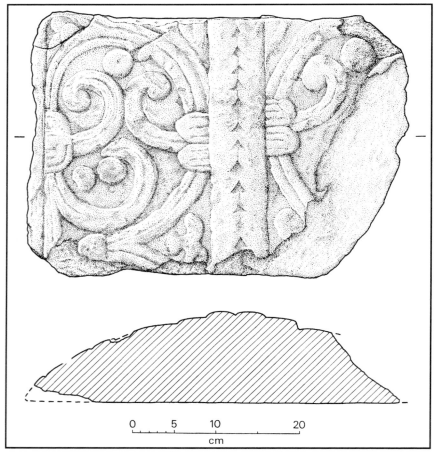

3. A piece of a late tenth-century limestone grave-cover, re-used in a twelfth-century stone burial cist. *(Drawing by Nick Griffiths)*

The precise location of the Saxon abbey church is still problematic, but at least it can be stated with confidence that it was definitely not to the south of the present church. Nor would there have sufficient room for it to the north, if the idea that Cheap Street was outside the Saxon precinct is correct. The early religious house is likely to have stood on the concrete platform, partially beneath the west end of the present church and following the alignment of the Roman temple precinct. But the lay-out of the cemetery indicates that in the tenth century, if not before, the Saxon monastery adopted an alignment

10° south of the Roman alignment, which was later retained by the Norman cathedral. It is almost certain that, like the Saxon abbey at Glastonbury,[21] it was directly beneath the nave of its Norman successor.

The Norman Cathedral Priory

After the death in 1088 of Giso, the last Saxon Bishop of Wells, the see was transferred to Bath. The abbey was transformed into a cathedral priory, and the new Norman Bishop of Bath, John of Tours, embarked on an ambitious building programme involving the construction of a massive cathedral (one of the largest, of its time, in England) and a Bishop's Palace. He also expanded the precinct so that it came to occupy most of the south-east quarter of the town.

The building campaign was evidently long drawn-out. The lower vaults were complete by 1122, when John died. He was buried in front of the High Altar, suggesting that work started at the east end, perhaps with the Saxon

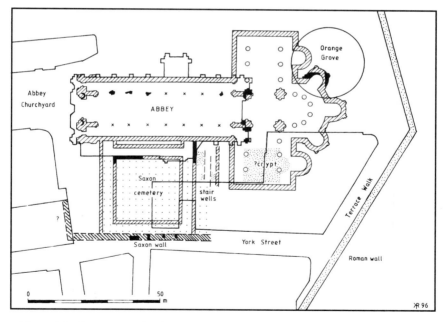

4. Plan of the Norman cathedral priory and the cloisters, overlying the late-Saxon cemetery. (*Drawing by Kirsty Rodwell*)

abbey being retained until the new presbytery was ready to be used for services. Further progress was made under Bishop Godfrey (1123-35) and after a major fire in 1137 his successor Robert of Lewes built the cloisters, chapter-house, refectory, dormitory and other parts of the priory complex. The cathedral may finally have been completed by 1156 when Papal confirmation of the transfer of the see from Wells to Bath was granted. The Norman church had a long life and survived until the start of the sixteenth century with only relatively minor structural alterations, such as Bishop Bytton's Lady Chapel, added on to the east end in the 1260s. It was then largely demolished and, due to the inspiration of Bishop King and Prior Bird, was replaced by the magnificent, but much shorter, present church. This was still incomplete in 1539 when the priory was dissolved.[22]

Apart from a few features such as the twelfth-century arch at the eastern end of the south aisle of the choir, still standing to its full height, most of what is known about the Norman nave is due to the remarkably detailed architectural and archaeological records made by James Irvine between 1863 and 1872, while employed as clerk of works during the restoration of the Abbey by Sir George Gilbert Scott. He planned all the Norman features revealed during the repairs and also drew an immaculate longitudinal section along the entire length of the present church showing, along with much else, the Norman floor in relation to its much higher Tudor replacement. In addition he recorded the tiled pavement in the central crossing, just beyond the east end of the present church.[23] Irvine was unable to investigate the transepts and the presbytery beyond the central crossing, and it was not until 1979 that part of a lateral apsidal side chapel was found during excavations beneath the circular lawn in Orange Grove. This discovery allowed a reconstruction of the plan of the east end of the cathedral to be made.[24]

However the shape of the transepts, as shown in the reconstructed plan, was based not on any hard evidence but on the reasonable assumption that they were built on the same module as the central crossing. In 1993, excavations on the south side of the church indicated that the south transept (and by implication the north transept as well) was larger than had previously been thought. A trench alongside the outer face of the south wall of the present choir confirmed Irvine's evidence not only that the sixteenth-century wall was built on the same line as its twelfth-century predecessor, but that in certain places the bases of Norman architectural features still survived *in situ*. Instead of the predicted west wall of the transept, on line with the west side of the central crossing, what was found was the base for the engaged shaft of an arch providing access from the west into the main body of the transept. The base of a second arch, with part of its shaft still intact, was also found immediately to the west, indicating that there had been an opening in the south wall of the Norman south aisle (fig. 5). The most likely explanation for these features is that the transept had a western aisle. A small part of the transept floor, consisting of two limestone slabs and a row of narrow plain glazed tiles, was observed, showing that the south transept floor was at the same level as the Norman nave. This is significant because, as Irvine demonstrated, the nave floor was 1ft 8ins (0.51m) below the level of the central crossing, which in turn was at least 10ins (0.25m) below the floor level of the north transept. So the floor level was stepped down from north to south.

5. An early-Norman engaged shaft in situ on the east side of the former opening between the south aisle of the Norman nave and the west aisle of the south transept, from the south. The paving is also Norman. The twelfth-century work survives within the foundations of the present, early sixteenth-century church. One-metre scale. (Photograph by Bath Archaeological Trust)

Further information can be gleaned about the plan of the transept from the important Terrace Walk excavations carried out by Bill Startin in 1973 in the garden between the Seventh Day Adventist chapel and the back of Whiteman's Bookshop.[25] In theory this should have located the east wall of the transept. In practice, graves in stone-capped cists were found on the line of the predicted wall. They were dated by Startin to the seventeenth century, but stylistically they are clearly medieval. The east wall of the transept must have been further to the east, suggesting that there was an eastern as well as a western aisle.

Of particular interest was a massive deep mortar-filled feature, only the curving north edge of which was recorded by Startin. It was interpreted at the time as the robber trench of the south wall of the Norman transept, but this interpretation is unlikely because the feature would have been almost in the centre of the transept. The explanation emerged in 1993 when excavations in the cellars under the pavement immediately north of Kingston Buildings found what must be the same feature. Its western edge was on a line with the arcade of the west aisle of the transept, and its base was 3m below the transept floor-level. It was filled in during the mid to late sixteenth century, after the Dissolution, and would appear to be a previously unidentified crypt, possibly with an apsidal east end. It occupied much of the area beneath the centre of the south transept and measured at least 14.5m x 11.5m. Its southern edge was not located but this must be beneath the houses at the eastern end of Kingston Buildings.

If the cathedral priory had followed the normal Benedictine plan, the east cloister walk ought to have been laid alongside the west wall of the transept. There is space for a passage in this position, but further west is a Norman building in a thoroughly unorthodox location. The stub end of its west wall, projecting out from beneath the south-east corner of the Rector's Vestry, was, inevitably, first spotted by Irvine. It had a plain chamfer on its outer (west) face, and although Irvine wrongly interpreted it as the west wall of the cloisters, he rightly identified it as Norman (fig. 6).[26] Further research in 1993 showed that the east wall of the Vestry, erected c.1615 in the angle between the early sixteenth-century south transept and the choir, incorporated much of the Norman wall. When the Vestry was constructed, the ground-level was considerably raised so that the new floor could be laid at a level nearer to that of the floor of the church. While the Vestry was temporarily closed for redecoration in 1993, the opportunity was taken to lift the wooden floor and to remove the Jacobean infill. In the process it was discovered that Irvine's Norman wall was still standing to a maximum height of 3.9m above the early-medieval ground-level. It sealed the late-Saxon burial horizon and had all the characteristics of an early twelfth-century wall. It was made of tightly-laid, coursed and diagonally-tooled limestone ashlar blocks, bonded in mortar identical to the matrix of the Norman features further east. Part of the wall face, from its base up to its highest surviving course, was reddened by intense burning, which may well have been caused by the fire of 1137.

6. The west wall of the early twelfth-century building projecting southwards from beneath the corner of the Jacobean Rector's Vestry. The one-metre scale rests on the wall's foundation raft, which is sealed beneath the remnants of the mid-twelfth-century east cloister walk. *(Photograph by Bath Archaeological Trust)*

A very short portion of the east wall was seen next to the present choir wall, showing that the building was c.10m wide externally. Investigations in the cellars in front of Kingston Buildings suggested it was at least 14m long. A strip of mortar bedding for a tile floor, c.2.5m wide, survived in the centre of the building, but most of the interior was occupied by two deep vertically-sided trenches running parallel and adjacent to the side walls. Each of these trenches was c.2.5m wide, and the bottom of the western one was 2.4m below the internal floor-level. The trenches were only filled in after the Dissolution, when the ashlar retaining walls were removed. The purpose of these features is unclear. They do not appear to have been part of an undercroft and one possibility is that they were stairwells providing access to and from a subterranean room, perhaps the crypt beneath the south transept. The position of the building is very puzzling and completely unorthodox, and its function is unknown, but it seems to have been erected at an early stage in the construction of the cathedral.

One question which remained outstanding until 1993 was the location of the Norman cloister walks. The early sixteenth-century plan is known because the openings from the church into the cloisters still exist. After the Reformation, when the Prior's lodgings were converted into a secular mansion, the walks served as garden paths, and are shown on seventeenth- and early eighteenth-century maps. But it was uncertain whether the cloisters, like the church, had been reduced in size during the Tudor rebuilding, or whether they had remained in the same place throughout the medieval period. This difficulty has now been resolved. Although some of the adjoining conventual buildings, such as the Prior's lodgings in the west range, were rebuilt, the line of the east, south and west walks remained unaltered from Robert of Lewes' time in the mid-twelfth century until the Dissolution. The only Tudor alteration was to the north walk, which was moved southwards to avoid the new south transept. The limestone paving of the east walk was found intact beneath and just to the south of the Rector's Vestry. On its east side, butting against the burnt part of the west wall of the earlier building, were the ashlar footings of a wall-bench. The junction with the north walk was also discovered. Again, the floor slabs were in place, directly overlain by the east wall of the present transept. Further south, within the cellars now occupied by the Abbey Heritage Centre, the floor of the east wall had been destroyed, but its line was indicated by a concentrated series of medieval graves packed in beneath the walk, clearly a much-favoured place of burial. Most of the north walk was inaccessible beneath the modern Choir Vestry, built adjacent to the south side of the church, but part of the south wall of the walk was recorded, as was the junction with the west walk. Most interesting of all was the south walk which, like the east walk, was indicated by medieval burials. Its southern edge was determined by the Saxon precinct wall. This wall, or a replacement on the same line, was incorporated in the Norman cloisters, and its foundations were only robbed out after the Dissolution. The walks enclosed a square cloister garth measuring c.24m across.

The Norman claustral complex adopted an unorthodox plan because it was constrained by pre-existing structures which were retained and incorporated within the new lay-out. The preservation of earlier structures, however inconvenient, certainly occurred elsewhere. At Wells Cathedral, the Chapel of St Mary, at the east end of the Saxon cathedral, was retained when the rest of the cathedral was demolished. It was converted into the Lady Chapel by the Cloister in the late twelfth century and was integrated with the new cloisters, despite being on a different alignment.[27] At Bath, the Saxon precinct wall is one example of a relict feature. Is it possible that the crypt beneath the south transept is a second example, Saxon in origin but preserved, for whatever reason, within the Norman cathedral?

The recent archaeological excavations have helped to solve a few long-standing problems about the plan of the cathedral priory, but at the same time have raised many new questions. For example, where were the monks housed before the mid-twelfth century? The suggestion that there was a massive temporary timber-framed complex is unconvincing;[28] it is much more likely that the conventual buildings of the late-Saxon abbey were retained until the new complex was built. If so, where were they located? Where was the Chapter House, the focal point of the administration of the priory? Was it next to the east cloister walk or was it sited to the south of the south transept? How was the lay-out of the monastic buildings affected by the relatively small size of the cloisters? Was the monks' dormitory built on a north-south alignment above the early-Norman structure next to the cloister walk, or could it have been aligned west-east between the cloisters and the transept? Was the dormitory, rebuilt by Bishop Bekynton in the mid-fifteenth century, a completely new structure or simply a modernization of the existing dormitory?

These and many other questions are worth posing even though some of them may be unanswerable because all but the deepest medieval layers are likely to have been destroyed by cellaring beneath the houses in Kingston Buildings and York Street. But a considerable amount of evidence survives beneath the pavement between Kingston Buildings and the Abbey, protected by an accumulation of post-medieval soil over 2m thick. Similarly, much of the plan of the east end of the cathedral and the north transept probably survives beneath Orange Grove. This essay is inevitably only an interim statement. As and when further archaeological excavations can be carried out, new information, not only about the Norman cathedral priory but also about the Saxon abbey and the origins of Christianity in Bath, will emerge and current ideas will undoubtedly have to be amended.

Notes

1   P. Davenport, 'Bath Abbey', *Bath History*, Vol. 2 (1988), pp.1-26.
2   J. Manco, 'The Buildings of Bath Priory', *Proceedings of Somerset Archaeological and Natural History Society*, Vol. 137 (1993), pp.75-109.
3   D.R. Walker, 'The Roman Coins', in B. Cunliffe, *The Temple of Sulis Minerva at Bath; the Finds from the Sacred Spring*, Vol. 2 (Oxford, 1988), pp.282-5.
4   B. Cunliffe and P. Davenport, *The Temple of Sulis Minerva at Bath; the Site*, Vol. 1 (Oxford, 1985), p.184.
5   A. Woodward, *Shrines and Sacrifices* (1992), pp.112-121.
6   P.J. Leach, 'The Roman Site at Fosse Lane, Shepton Mallet', *Proceedings of Somerset Archaeological and Natural History Soc.*, Vol. 134 (1990), p.51, plate 1.
7   A. Woodward, *Shrines and Sacrifices*, pp.96-7.
8   M.Aston, 'The Bath Region from Late Prehistory to the Middle Ages', *Bath History*, Vol. 1 (1986), p.73.
9   B. Cunliffe and P. Davenport, *The Temple of Sulis Minerva at Bath; the Site*, Vol. 1, pp.184-5.
10   A. Woodward and P. Leach, *The Uley Shrines* (1993), p.11 and fig.9.
11   B. Cunliffe, *Roman Bath* (1968), pp.148-9, figs. 26 and 30.
12   M.Aston, 'The Bath Region from Late Prehistory to the Middle Ages', pp.73-7.
13   M.Aston, *Monasteries* (1993), pp.30-4; and 'Llandough', *Current Archaeology*, Vol. 13, No. 2 (Jan. 1996), pp.73-5.
14   J. Manco, 'The Buildings of Bath Priory', pp.75-7.
15   J.T. Irvine, 'Description of the remains of the Norman Cathedral of Bath', *Journal of British Archaeological Association*, 1st series, Vol. 46 (1890), p.85; E. Holland and M. Chapman, *The Story of the White Hart Inn* (Bath, 1990).
16   A. Vince, 'Swallow Street: the medieval and post-medieval pottery', in P. Davenport ed., *Archaeology in Bath 1976-1985* (Oxford, 1991), p.72.
17   V. Russett and W.J. Rodwell, personal communication.
18   B. Cunliffe and P. Davenport, *The Temple of Sulis Minerva at Bath; the Site*, Vol. 1, p.185, and plates XXIX and XXX.
19   P. Rahtz, *Glastonbury* (1993), pp.92-4.
20   B. Cunliffe, *The City of Bath* (Gloucester, 1986), p.59.
21   P. Rahtz, *Glastonbury*, fig.44.
22   P. Davenport, 'Bath Abbey', pp.7-8, 11-15, 20-2.
23   J.T. Irvine, 'Description of the remains of the Norman Cathedral of Bath', pp.85-94; Bath Central Library, Irvine papers, Vol. 5.
24   T.J. O'Leary, 'Excavations at Orange Grove and Related Studies', in P. Davenport ed., *Archaeology in Bath 1976-1985*, pp.32-8.
25   B. Startin, 'Excavations at Terrace Walk 1973', in B. Cunliffe (ed.), *Excavations in Bath 1950-1975* (CRAAGS, 1979), pp.94-101.
26   J.T. Irvine, 'Description of the remains of the Norman Cathedral of Bath', p.93.
27   W.J. Rodwell, 'The Anglo-Saxon and Norman Churches at Wells', in L. Colchester ed., *Wells Cathedral* (Shepton Mallet, 1982), pp.15-17.
28   J. Manco, 'The Buildings of Bath Priory', pp.87-9 and fig.2.

THE BARTON OF BATH

A.J. Keevil

In the south-western counties, the term 'barton' (Latin *bertona*) was used in the medieval period to refer to the home farm or demesne (domain) of the lord of a manor. The Bath Barton was the agricultural demesne of the lord of the manor of Bath, which belonged to the king. Large monastic demesne farms were generally known as 'granges', and the Barton farm, held of the Crown over a long period by Bath Priory, was frequently described as the 'Grange or manor of Barton'. The Barton name acquired a wider significance when it came also to be given to the 'hundred' (the unit of administration within the shire) surrounding Bath. This large rural area was originally called the 'hundred of Bath', but because it lay ouside the city, and had the Barton as its chief manor, came to be known as the *'forinsecum* [or 'foreign'] hundred of the Barton of Bath', later abbreviated to 'Bathforum hundred'. The present article attempts to examine the complex subject of the Barton within an historical framework, and in the light of its location and topography, the nature of the farming practised, the various forms of tenure and the range of individuals involved, as well as the relationship with the city, with Walcot, and with the hundred.

At Domesday, Bath (assessed at 20 hides, with a fiscally appended two-hide estate at Batheaston) and its hundred (of 95 hides) belonged to the king, to whom it had reverted upon the death in 1074 of Queen Edith, who had held it, probably as a dower from her husband, Edward the Confessor.[1] Although Domesday records mention neither the Barton beside Bath nor Walcot, in which Barton Grange lay, they were probably included in the 20 hides of Bath (for which no agrarian details are given).

The city itself, probably from Saxon times, embraced, in addition to the walled area, only the parish of St Michael without, and the external part of the parish of St James (within the southern loop of the river). This was also the city area in 1379.[2] Even in the eighteenth century, it was the full extent of the jurisdiction of the Court of Record of the city, and, c.1690, the limits of the city charged for tax, despite a boundary extension in 1590, embracing part of Walcot.[3]

The external 'hundred of Bath' (called, in the thirteenth century, 'the foreign hundred of the Barton of Bath,[4] and later 'Bathforum hundred') contained eighteen present-day parishes surrounding the city. At

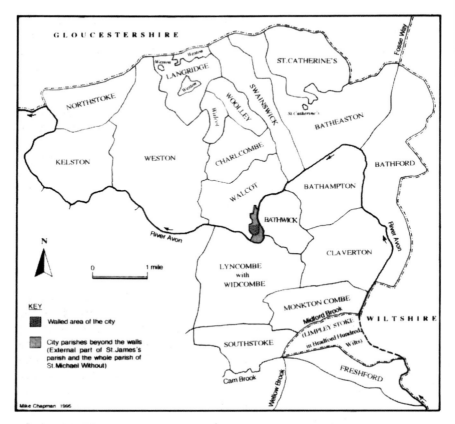

1. 'The hundred of Bath', alias 'the foreign hundred of the Barton of Bath', alias 'the hundred of Bathforum'.

Domesday, manors in thirteen of them (some parishes containing more than one manor) were listed, and were apparently in the 'hundred of Bath'.[5] There seems little doubt that whatever the reason for the omission of St Catherine,[6] Kelston, Northstoke, Southstoke and Walcot, they too would have been within the orbit of Bath and its hundred at Domesday.

The Hundred of Bath: possible origins and extent

The 'hundred of Bath' (as it was known at Domesday) is generally considered to owe its origin to the 'hundred *manentes*' (or hides) 'adjacent to the city of Hat Bathu' granted in 676 by Osric, king of Hwiccia (a sub-

kingdom of Mercia in which Bath then lay), to found there, under the
abbess Bertana, a nunnery (later becoming the Bath Monastery of St Peter),
as detailed in a somewhat dubious copy of the foundation charter.[7]
Although there was also a 'hundred of Barton by Bristol' (its Barton manor
being regarded in the mid-thirteenth century as the demesne farm of
Bristol Castle), there may be a closer analogy with the 'hundred of Barton
by Gloucester', and Osric's foundation of St Peter's there.[8] Finberg indicated
the likelihood of the long continuation, through British and into Mercian
times, of the Roman form of the Gloucester, Cirencester and Bath estates,
because of the convenience, in a highly romanized area, of inheriting an
efficient Roman taxation system.[9] More recently, Aston suggested that
the area that became Bathforum hundred may represent the survival of
an early multiple estate, of Roman or even pre-Roman origin.[10]

Earliest References to the Barton

Neither Barton nor Walcot, or even the 'hundred', is mentioned in the
series of Crown charters, between 1090 and 1111, which moved the seat
of the bishopric to Bath, and granted John de Villula and the Abbey of
St Peter all the Abbey possessions in the city and beyond, the whole
city itself, its hidage of 20 hides, and all its internal and external
appurtenances.[11] However a subsequent Crown charter (undated, but pre-
1135), and papal bulls of Adrian, 1156, and Alexander III, 1178, together
prove that the 'appurtenances' had included the Barton (named in the
last) and jurisdiction over 'the entire hundred of Bath', its manors having
to pay suit at the bishop's court.[12] In 1135, Bishop Robert, in confirming
restorations made by his predecessors of ancient Abbey possessions to
the priory, also added 'the full tithe of Barton and Lyncombe' and 'the
tithe of my vineyards of Lyncombe and Beckenofna' (the latter being the
Barton 'Vineyards' in Walcot).[13] The Barton was evidently held, with the
city and hundred, in the bishop's hands.

Later, Bishop Reginald (1174-92) granted one and a half virgates of land
in Shockerwick to Richard de Ford, to serve as 'hundredman' (bailiff) of
the 'hundred of Bath' and have all customs and rights belonging to such
office.[14] The *Pipe Roll* for Michaelmas 1197[15] confirms that Richard de Ford
had 'the manor of Bath to farm' (receiving payment of ten marks), paying
the total annual rent of £42 16s 10d, so it presumably included the Barton
and hundred, although again not specifically mentioned (but see the *Pipe*

Roll of 1195, below). Cam observed that 'the office of bailliff of the hundred of Bath was hereditary and attached to the tenure of a piece of land'.[16] Of interest, therefore, is a grant of 1343 concerning 'the manor of Shockerwick, together with the bailiwick of the bedelry of the hundred of Bathforum, and the rents and reversions of all tenants, both free and others, in Walcot, Langridge and Bath'[17] (all three having Barton relevance, see below).

In 1194, Bishop Savaric exchanged with Richard I, the city of Bath for Glastonbury Abbey.[18] The exchange evidently included the Barton, because at Michaelmas 1195 the account for 'firma de Bada et Berton' appears in the 'Roll of Escheats',[19] thus indicating that Bath and the Barton were then in the king's hands. The inclusion also of the 'foreign' hundred is confirmed by the thirteenth-century jurors' statement, that 'King John [r. 1199-1216] ... held [implying 'in his hands', as the property belonged to the Crown] the city of Bath with the suburb of Barton outside the city, with the rent, services and all other things of its "foreign" hundred'.[20]

Bath Priory obtains the Barton

In 1204, King John granted specifically to Bath Priory 'our Barton outside the city, with the whole of the "foreign" hundred belonging to it, in perpetual free alms, at a fee farm rent of twenty pounds per annum'.[21] He also granted it the city of Bath 'at his pleasure', for £30 per annum.[22] Although the 'foreign' (Barton) hundred thus came under the prior's jurisdiction from 1204, and so remained until the Dissolution, the men of certain Bath 'foreign' lands were withdrawn from suit at the hundred court: by the Earls of Gloucester (father and son in succession), in respect of Langridge and Freshford (eventually returned), and by Bishop Jocelyn, in respect of several other manors.[23] The prior had in fact conceded to the bishop, in 1232/3, that the men of some of these lands, who had formerly done suit at the prior's 'hundred of Bath', should in future do suit 'at the bishop's hundred of Hampton' (Bathampton).[24] These possessions of the bishop became known as the 'liberties of Hampton and Claverton' (both formerly part of the 'prior's hundred of Bath') and continued to be so styled until comparatively recent times.[25]

Thirteenth-century cartulary entries and fourteenth-century documents show that lessees in the prior's manors of the 'foreign' hundred were required to do 'suit of court at the two hundreds de la Berton' (i.e. attend the hundred court at Hockday and Michaelmas, yearly) and generally also suit 'twice yearly' at the court leet of the manor in question.[26] In the thirteenth century, there are also references to the 'Hundred de la Buri' (probably referring to the 'hundred' or 'liberty' of the borough or city area) and to the 'entire hundred of Bath' (probably embracing both city and 'foreign' hundreds).[27] Unfortunately, no court rolls under the names of 'Berton' or 'Barton' (beside Bath), nor yet of 'Bathforum' have been found.[28] Although Lambeth Palace Library hold 'hundred and hallmote rolls' of 1361, 1382, 1421 and 1432 for *Civitas Bathon*,[29] they appear to deal with the city area only (limits given above) – the thirteenth-century 'hundred de la Buri'.

Even after 1204, when the Priory held the Barton (with the *forinsecum* hundred) at fee farm, Bath citizens retained their right of common upon it. After some disagreement the Priory, in 1260, admitted the citizens' rights 'in Kingsmead' (Barton meadow) and 'in the stubble fields pertaining to the Barton' (see below); and again, in 1345, the Priory confirmed their rights, 'despite the sowing that year of the Hayes [see below] within our manor of Barton',[30] thus demonstrating the continued close association of the city with its demesne farm. Disputes continued even after the Dissolution, and the Corporation produced these medieval documents as proof of their rights, until the matter was finally settled by arbitration in 1619 (see below).

The 1260 agreement shows that the citizens were to pasture their cattle in Kingsmead from 1 August until the prior put his cattle into the Barton stubble fields (West or East Fields, depending upon the year of cultivation), when they must do likewise with their cattle, but remove them to Kingsmead again from 25 October until 30 November. The citizens' cattle were not allowed in any 'anciently enclosed' Barton grounds until the prior's had pastured there for three consecutive weeks. Various small charges ($\frac{1}{2}$d, 1d, $1\frac{1}{2}$d) per head of cattle were levied.

Evidence suggests that Bath with the Barton (and its 'foreign' hundred) had been a traditional royal dower. It is evident that Queen Edith had held Bath with its hundred (and also therefore, presumably, the Barton) from before the Conquest (see above). When Henry III granted the city of Bath in dower to his queen, Eleanor, in 1236, the phrase '*cum pertinenciis suis*' probably implied the inclusion of the Barton with its 'foreign' hundred.[31] Certainly, on coming to the throne (1273), their son, Edward I, assigned 'the city of Bath with the Barton and with all its other appurtenances' to 'Eleanor, the king's mother, in dower'[32] as though it were simply a renewal. Thus she continued to benefit from the fee farm Crown rents, totalling £50 (see also below).

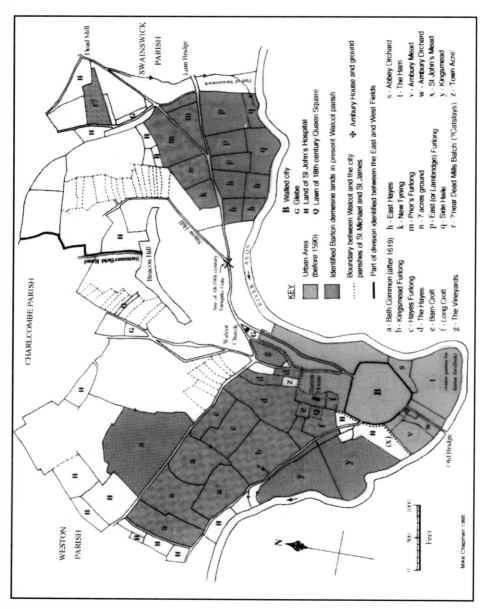

2. The former urban area of Bath (until 1590) and the parish of Walcot, based on Thorpe's *Plan of the Parish of Walcot*, 1740.

In 1275, Bishop Robert regained from the king (on surrendering Glastonbury Abbey to him) 'the city of Bath and the suburbs ... without any retention except the Barton [and its 'foreign' hundred] which the prior and convent [already] hold in fee farm'.[33] The bishop was also granted £53 annually from the revenues of 'the royal barton of Bath and the royal manor of Congresbury'.[34] The re-exchange particularly mentioned 'the meadow of the city towards the east' (i.e. 'the Ham' in St James's parish). Later evidence (see below) shows that the 'Eweflock of Barton' had winter pasturage rights on 'the Ham'.

As the city had been granted to the bishop 'free and quit of all secular service', the prior (still the tenant) was no longer liable for its annual rent of £30, but only for the Barton rent of £20.[35] Consequently, the queen mother surrendered the city of Bath, 'saving to her the barton', and was granted in exchange 'the town and mills of Rye in dower', to the same value.[36] However, after her death, Edward I, in 1299, 'assigned in dower to Margaret, sister of Philip, king of France' (to whom he had become betrothed) 'in accordance with the treaty, Bath town and Barton, the "farm" of £20 paid for these' – the £30 for the city being no longer payable.[37] In 1411, Edmund of Woodstock's heirs were still inheriting 'the farm of £20 ... for the town of Bath and the Berton', granted to him in 1319.[38]

Walcot Township and Barton Grange

There is clear evidence of a Roman settlement in Walcot, near the river crossing (and of Bronze Age occupation near by).[39] A nucleated Saxon village may have existed there. Its name, as with other Walcots, similarly situated near important settlements, probably means 'cottages of the serfs'; its later inhabitants certainly owed service on the Bath Barton (see below).[40] The earliest cartulary reference to Walcot church, which (as shown) 'stands on Barton land' (and beside the Fosseway), is c.1198-1223.[41] Its foundation may have been Saxon, for it stands in the vicinity of the principal Roman cemetery, and furthermore, its former name, mentioned in 1535, was 'All Hallows', apparently indicative of ancient dedication.[42] There were eleven householders in Walcot, in 1327.[43] From 1501 until at least 1641, the number remained constant at about twenty.[44] *The Plan of Walcot*, 1740, shows a 'ribbon development' of dwellings, beginning on both sides of the church, converging in the London Road, and extending as far as the turnpike gate (at the foot of the present Snow Hill).

Barton House or Farmhouse (containing a 'courthouse' – see below), although in Walcot parish, lay close to the city and is shown on seventeenth-century maps.[45] Its site now forms the north-east end of John Street (at the rear of Jolly's), facing into King Street, the farmyard occupying the present Barton Court.[46] Before 1768, the farmhouse had been converted into two messuages, later numbered 9 & 10 King Street, and so remained into the mid-nineteenth century.[47]

A curious complaint was made, 1274-6, 'that the grange and oxhouse of Barton belonging to the lord the king has been removed [*distracta*] and placed [*allocata*] elsewhere in the territory of the prior'.[48] Whether this referred to a physical or fiscal re-allocation is not clear, but possible removal from the vicinity of the township to the above site cannot be ruled out. The 'office of farm bailiff of the manor de la Berton without Bath' was granted to Geoffrey, son of William and Edith Newman, by Prior Thomas (c.1332-40).[49] The bailiff would have dwelt in the manor house (Barton House), directed the husbandry of the demesne and its stock, and rendered a yearly account for the whole manor.[50]

The inhabitants of Walcot (eleven in 1327 – see above) were the customary tenants of the manor who owed service upon the Barton demesne. In the fourteenth century, here as elsewhere, there is evidence of peasant rebellion, and in 1378 the king empowered action against the long-term refusal of customs and services by (*inter alia*) the prior of Bath's tenants of Barton and Batheaston.[51] In 1380, two tenants brought an action against the prior for exacting unlawful customs at Barton.[52]

In 1501, one Walcot tenant held a 'virgate' (quarter hide) and house (rent 26/8d p.a.); eighteen others held 'farndell' (quarter virgate) tenements (mostly 5/11½d p.a.).[53] Several tenants also held small acreages of 'bordland' (i.e. discarded demesne – called 'overland', when taken out by the prior in 1385),[54] totalling 24 acres altogether, mostly in the West Field. In addition, over 30 acres of Barton demesne, much of it pasture/meadow (including a 'piece of meadow within Barton Furlong' and therefore formerly arable), were also let in small parcels to tenants by 1501.

A rental of c.1600 shows that the 'virgate' holding (rent unchanged from 1501) was unusually large, containing 59 acres 5 rods, excluding 'overland'.[55] The majority of 'farndell' holdings varied between 9½ and 12 acres. Each holding consisted of scattered, small plots, generally of between half an acre and two acres, some much smaller. In only a few cases is 'arable' specified or implied, and in only one holding was it evenly distributed between the two Fields.[56] However, some conversion from arable to pasture, as had occurred elsewhere between c.1340s and 1500,[57] may partly explain this, because the plot locations suggest a more even distribution between the two Fields. A fossilised form of the pattern of tenants' plots is still apparent in Thorpe's *Plan* of 1740.

Generation after generation of the Saunders family (always multiple holders) remained tenants of the 'virgate' (later combined with two particular 'farndell' holdings), at least between 1501 and 1641.[58] The 'farndell' called 'Chitters' descended through another branch. From 1623, yet another Saunders held a 'farndell' tenement, together with some Barton demesne. 'Heriot' (death duty) for the 'virgate' was 'best beast or 4/-'; for many of the 'farndell' tenements '1/8d'. The 'virgate' holding had 'common' for 18 bullocks and 180 sheep; three 'farndell' holdings for 3 bullocks and 30 sheep each.

There are references to both 'Manor of Walcot' (see below) and 'Manor of Barton' (see above), but it seems doubtful whether there were separate manor courts. In Ministers' Accounts, 1539, 'perquisites of court' are shown for 'Walcot' (manor), and for 'Hundred of Barton', but not for 'Barton [Manor or Grange] with rectory'. There exist rolls of 'hallmotes of Walcot', 1309-1502, but not in unbroken sequence;[59] it has already been seen that no 'hallmote' or 'hundred' rolls under the name of 'Berton' or 'Barton' beside Bath have been found.

It can be shown that both before and after the Dissolution, Barton matters were treated in the manor court of Walcot. In a Walcot hallmote extract of 22 September 1518, is an order 'to all' forbidding certain grazing 'in the stubble fields' after 1 August, under a penalty 'anciently imposed by the lord', and a further order 'to all the tenants of Walcot' not to graze sheep 'in les Hayes in the East Field and in Side Heil ... under penalty of a fine of 40d'.[60] The 'stubble fields' in Walcot belonged to the Barton (see the prior's agreement of 1260) and both 'les Hayes in the East Field' and 'Side Heil' were demesne grounds. Long after the Dissolution, in 1616, the lessee of 49 acres, 'which said premises are parcel of the Farm of Barton', was to do 'suit at the lessor's court of Walcot when holden'.[61] Again, in 1635, some leased Barton grounds were described as being 'within the manor of Walcot' and the lessee was not only 'to do suit' at the lessor's court there, but the rent was to be paid 'in or at their farmhouse called Barton Farmhouse'.[62] Possibly the terms 'hallmote de la Berton' (used in 1331)[63] and 'hallmote of Walcot' were synonymous.

The open two-field system operated throughout Bathforum hundred.[64] In 1260 (and probably long before), Walcot had West and East Fields 'pertaining to the Barton', cultivated alternately, year by year, and Bath citizens had common pasturage rights on them after harvest. The system continued into the early seventeenth century but reference to the West and East Fields was still being made in 1737, although building developments had already begun there, and continued apace in the late eighteenth century.

According to a MS of c.1612, concerning citizens' rights of common, the West and East Fields, 'parcels' of Barton farm, contained about 250 and 200 acres respectively.[65] 'The Hayes' (an ancient Barton enclosure) of about 25 acres, although in the West Field, was nevertheless always cultivated with the East Field (perhaps to balance the acreages). Unlike tenants' scattered allocations, the demesne arable occupied blocks divided into 'furlongs' (some anciently enclosed – see below) within the Fields. 'Sopers', in the former detached part of Walcot on Lansdown (see below), was described as lying 'in the north-east part of the West Field' and 'anciently' enclosed with a stone wall, containing 'about 50 acres', partly woodland. 'Within the circuit' of the West and East Fields, the Walcot Manor tenants held about 100 acres in each; St John's Hospital about 20 in the former and 12 in the latter; while the king held 4 in the former and 12 in the latter; these other lands also had been 'always subject and open to this common', although some were enclosed by c.1612.

Unfortunately the earliest available map of Walcot gives no indication of the division between the two Fields.[66] The prior's agreement of 1260 suggests that the East Field of Barton lay 'between Walcot' (the township) 'and the bridge of Lambridge' (on London Road, at the eastern end of the parish). Since the West and East Fields 'adjoined one another',[67] the division possibly passed north-south through the township (unless the 1260 description referred only to 'East Field demesne'). North of Beacon Hill, the present Summerfield Road (part of a direct route to 'the down' and 'Sopers') divided grounds identifiable as lying in opposite Fields.[68] Similar identifications south of Beacon Hill have so far proved elusive. Thus the division there remains uncertain, although its line must have run west of 'Coffin's Batch' (No.126 on Thorpe's *Plan* of 1740), identified as in the East Field.[69] However, if the 1260 description referred only to the East Field demesne, the Field division may have run much further west, perhaps along a route (including Summerfield Road) centred on the farmyard, a not uncommon arrangement, except that in Walcot, farm and township are so far apart.

Although certain pieces of Barton demesne had clearly been leased by the Priory to sub-tenants, even before 1331 (when they were again leased to a Bath family for lives, in succession to another), the earliest known Priory lease of Barton Grange itself (including Kingsmead, the Hayes, Sopers, Lipwell and the Eweflock of Barton consisting of 360 sheep) is that of 2 January 1518 to Henry Bewshin.[70] Previously it had probably been kept 'in hand' by the Priory and under the management of their bailiff. Bewshin's lease was renewed on 2 January 1529 and included his wife and sons, William and Peter (for lives, at a rent of £18 p.a.).[71] However, even in 1515/16, Henry Bewshin had held the Barton Eweflock, while Nicholas Saunders (probably son of William of the Walcot 'virgate' of 1501) held the Barton cattle (5 cows, 10 oxen, 2 steers, 1 heifer and 4 calves).[72] By the lease of 1529, Henry Bewshin (with wife and sons) also held 'the whole rectory of Barton' for lives, at a rent of £10 p.a.[73] The 'rectory of Barton' refers to the Barton tithes in the parish of Walcot. The lessee was required to keep in repair the chancel of Walcot Church and to pay 53/4d in augmentation of the vicar's stipend.[74]

Minister's Accounts for 1539 show Henry Bewshin as 'farmer' of Barton Grange and Rectory, and collector/bailiff of Walcot (the latter office probably in succession to Thomas Batyn).[75] After the Dissolution, Henry Bewshin, followed by his son and grandson, in succession, continued to hold both Barton Grange with the Eweflock and Barton Rectory (paying rent to those who held 'in chief').

Post-Dissolution Developments

After the Dissolution, the 'foreign' hundred of the Barton of Bath (Bathforum hundred) became the subject of quite separate Crown grants from those of the Grange of Barton. Initially granted in 1541 to Edward, Earl of Hertford,[76] it passed through many hands. A Parliamentary Survey of 4 May 1652 states that the sheriff's (twice-yearly) 'tourns' of the hundred (although 'much discontinued ... for divers years past') were held 'under an ash-tree on Odwood's Down [now Odd Down] on the north side of the Fosseway from Bath to Wells in the parish of Englishcombe [just outside the Bathforum hundred and probably indicative of Bath's former much larger area of jurisdiction], but in wet weather, in the court-house in Barton Grange'.[77]

In 1791, it was stated that 'the hundred of Bathforum is divided between two high constables, and has for its lord, William Oliver, MD [a descendant of the Dr Oliver of 'Oliver Biscuit' fame], who holds his court in Widcombe' (almost certainly an error for 'Weston', the manor held with the hundred, since 1759, by the Olivers, and from at least 1612, by their predecessors).[78] Although this suggests that the hundred court was then being held in the courthouse of Weston manor, no corroborating evidence has been discovered. In the early nineteenth century, until it ceased functioning, an annual court leet of Bathforum hundred (which by that time, inexplicably, included the city parishes, as confirmed by the 1841 census) appears to have been held at the Pulteney Hotel, Bath.[79] The separate identity of the 'Liberty of Hampton and Claverton' apparently continued until 1869.[80]

In 1547, Edward VI granted Sir William Herbert 'the grange and farm called Barton next Bath and all its demesne lands in the parishes of Lyncombe, Widcombe, Walcot and Barton ... all closes adjacent to the said grange and all the demesne lands and works of customary tenants of Walcot and Barton and of other inhabitants within the hundred of Barton',[81] formerly priory property. The grant included 'the Eweflock of Barton' of 360 sheep and their pasturage in Walcot, Barton, Lyncombe and Widcombe, leased with the grange to Henry Bewshin and family; and 'the Hogg Flock' (yearlings) of 322 sheep and their pasturage in Lyncombe and Widcombe, in the tenure of Robert and Richard Cox ('Cockes'). Some eighteen lands in 'Lyncombe, Widcombe, Walcot and Barton' are named in the grant (including three in the parish of St James and four in the former detached part of Walcot on Lansdown), as well as Warleigh Wood in Bathford. It is doubtful whether Warleigh Wood, the Hogg Flock and two grounds (Ambury Mead and Orchard) in St James's were Barton properties; the Ham there provided winter pasture for the Barton Flock (see below).

Barton Grange was conveyed by Sir William Herbert (in exchange for other property) to Matthew Colthurst in 1548.[82] The conveyance included courts-leet and view of frankpledge (i.e. the 'lordship of Walcot'), advowson (of Walcot Church), fishing, etc. The property was held in chief of the Crown, by service of one-twentieth part of a knight's fee, paying yearly 'for the aforesaid grange and farm and other premises in Barton 29/4d, and for the aforesaid pasture and other premises in Lyncombe and Widcombe 16/9d' – with no further mention of Warleigh Wood. There had also been a Crown grant of 1543 to Matthew Colthurst of the site of the late Priory of Bath with closes 'le Ham' and 'Ambrye Meade' in St James's parish and lands (named) in Lyncombe, Widcombe, Holloway and Walcot, and works of customary tenants there, and the chief messuage of (Monkton) Combe ... all of which belonged to Bath Priory.[83] Certain Priory lands provided pasture for Barton stock and thus are named also in the Barton documents.

Edmund Colthurst, son and heir of Matthew (died 8 July 1559), inherited all the Barton property, as detailed in the conveyance of 1548, as well as the site of the former Priory and its property (including his residence, Abbey House, adjoining the Abbey), granted in 1543. He sold Barton

Grange (then in the occupation of William Sherston, son-in-law of Peter Bewshin, son of Henry, and the inheritor of the sub-tenure under the Colthursts) in 1591 to Sir George Snigg.[84] Although the sale included the detached part of Walcot on Lansdown, Snigg did not obtain 'the Ham' (but only the winter feeding for the Eweflock there), nor any of the Lyncombe property. Fragmentation had begun.

By 1612, Colthurst had sold to a John Hall of Bradford-on-Avon, most Priory property in the city (but had given the Abbey Church to the Corporation in 1572), including 'the Ham' meadow and also the Lyncombe and Widcombe property.[85] These items passed through several generations of John Halls and, by the marriage of the heiress of the last, to the Dukes of Kingston. In the eighteenth century, Ralph Allen acquired Prior Park and all the pasture in Lyncombe and Widcombe, paying the Crown rent of 16/9d.[86]

William Snigg, son and heir of Sir George (died 11 December 1617), inherited his father's Barton Grange property and Barton rectory (the latter purchased by his father from the Crown lessees in 1612),[87] and also the Manor of Walcot (probably not acquired by his father until c.1611 – see below). However, in 1635, being in serious financial difficulties, William assigned Barton Grange, including Kingsmead (particularly mentioned), and all his other property in Walcot and Bath to Mary Jackson, his sister, for 80 years, on her undertaking to repay his debts.[88] He then obtained Crown licences to sell to Thomas Haines, in 1638 and 1639, seven grounds of Barton Grange, and Haines became responsible for paying 12/4d of the annual Crown rent.[89] The Haines family still held their Barton property in 1740.[90]

When Peter Bewshin was sub-tenant of Barton, the Corporation had agreed, in 1570, to forfeit their rights of common, only in the 'ancient enclosures' (with the exception of Kingsmead), provided he paid them 40/- yearly.[91] In a later, long-running dispute with the Sniggs (as tenants-in-chief) concerning the citizens' rights on the Barton, the Corporation produced the agreements of 1260 and 1345 to support their claim. The matter was finally settled, after arbitration, in 'the Award' of 1619 by which, 'in lieu of indefinite rights of common', the citizens were to have in perpetuity, on payment of 40/- annual rent to William Snigg and his heirs, nearly 100 acres (in the West Field) of Barton Farm, to be designated 'the Bath Common'[92] – the present High, Middle and Lower Commons, the Botanical Gardens and the Children's Playground.

In 1621, William Snigg sold the winter feeding which 'the occupiers of Barton ... had by custom and usage in the Ham ... ' (for the Eweflock) to William Sherston,[93] the occupier of Barton Farm in 1591 (see above). What happened to the Eweflock is not known. It does not appear in Snigg's existing rental and survey of 1623-41.[94] He may have sold it to Sherston. The last oblique reference to it and its shepherd is in the Walcot Glebe Terrier of 1606, which states that the shepherd was allowed to keep the tithe of twenty sheep (of the Barton Eweflock).[95] In an eighteenth-century enquiry regarding 'the Ham', it was remembered by one aged citizen that there had been 'a report of a sheep common in the winter, but of what nature or to whom belonging ... [he] never knew or heard'.[96] It would seem that the Eweflock had long ceased to exist.

By 1656, Thomas Saunders the elder, of Beechwood, Herts, was 'lord of the manor of Walcot'.[97] A lease of 1660 states that he possessed the land in Walcot in the right of his wife Mary, for about 55 years yet to come.[98] She may, therefore, have been the daughter and heiress of Mary Jackson (the sister of William Snigg, to whom the latter had assigned his property in 1635 for 80 years). Thomas Saunders was perhaps of the family who had held the 'virgate' and other Walcot holdings during several generations. In 1681, William Hooper, the purchaser of certain Walcot lands, was ' to do suit at the court of William Saunders [possibly the son of Thomas] holden for the manor of Walcot'.[99] A deed of common recovery, dated 10 October 1687, shows that a William Saunders (perhaps of the next generation) then acquired the inheritable freehold of the lordship of Walcot and rectory of Walcot, the latter being the Barton tithes.[100] That he had also acquired Snigg's unsold parts of Barton Grange is clear, as the inheritance included the annual rent payable by Bath Corporation for 'Bath Common' (formerly Barton land – as above).

On 16 June 1699, William Saunders sold the Manor and Rectory of Walcot, with appurtenances, courts, etc., 'except Barton Farm' (which he had already conveyed to two gentlemen, in trust 'to certain uses') and except a number of Walcot tenant holdings (sold in five separate lots, the largest share to his bailiff, William Hooper, in 1681 – as above), to Robert Gay, surgeon, of London (who married Mary, daughter of William Saunders).[101] In the early eighteenth century, Robert Gay had apparently also come into possession of Barton Farm,[102] probably by virtue of his wife's inheritance, arranged by her father, when he had conveyed the farm in trust 'to certain uses'. When Robert Gay died in 1737, he left the Bath property to his daughter Margaret, by his second wife. She died without issue in 1765 and left the estate to her brother-in-law, Sir Benet Garrard who, in 1767, bequeathed all his Bath estate to Sir Peter Rivers, who took the name of Gay. The ground rents were sold after the death of Sir Henry Chandos Rivers, in 1870.[103]

Throughout the sixteenth century, various Bewshin family members in succession occupied, as under-tenants, the Barton Grange property (detailed in the Priory lease of 1518 as above). By the early seventeenth century, the Barton demesne was divided into a number of separate sub-tenures. John Chapman, apparently then the principal under-tenant (when William Snigg held Barton Grange 'in chief' of the Crown), further sub-let Barton Farmhouse, its outbuildings and some demesne grounds in the West Field only to another man.[104] The rest of the demesne was leased in a number of separate lots. Snigg's leases of Barton demesne are listed in his rentals and survey of 1623-41 quite separately from those of his Walcot tenants' lands (shown as 'the manor' held by him 'in socage').

The rental of 1623 distinguishes the acreages of arable from those of pasture/meadow in each of the various holdings. In total there were then 360 acres of arable (Barton demesne, 176 acres; Walcot tenants' land, 184 acres); and 362 acres of meadow/pasture (Barton demesne, 244 acres; Walcot tenants' land, 118 acres). Much of the Barton demesne then consisted of six (named) 'furlongs' (originally, therefore, arable but some converted to pasture) of about 20 or 25 acres each, within the two Fields, and also the large meadow of Kingsmead (48 acres). In some cases the furlongs had become divided into two or four closes by 1623.

The 1623 rental shows that one furlong (then in two closes) and two other closes (converted to pasture) were to be ploughed for two years only (departing from alternate-year cultivation), while another furlong (converted to pasture) was 'not to be ploughed'. Youings has observed that, in the West Country generally, little monastic demesne was leased until c.1500, but leasing steadily progressed thereafter.[105] She also noted that conversion of arable to pasture had often begun earlier, and short-term ploughing of pasture also occurred. The Barton evidence suggests a similar pattern at Bath.

Although 'court-leet and view of frank-pledge, heriots', etc., were included in the conveyance of Barton Grange to Colthurst in 1548, they were not specifically mentioned in the 1591 conveyance to Snigg. In fact, in 1571 Peter Bewshin (son of Henry and inheritor of the Barton Grange tenancy, under those who held *in capite*) obtained a Crown lease of Walcot manor for 21 years. Peter died in 1584. In 1590, Robert Chambers (for many years Town Clerk of Bath) became 'lord of the manor of Walcot', probably for 21 years, thus terminating c.1611. Sir George Snigg may then have obtained the lordship. William (his son and heir) certainly held it 'in socage' (as well as 'a parcel of Barton Farm *in capite*') and received the rents and services, besides being entitled to 'heriots'. William Snigg must have held the manor in perpetuity, as he made calculations for selling the individual

tenancies at 20 years' purchase.[106] Subsequent holders of the lordship (and
of 'a parcel of Barton Farm') appear to have derived it from the Sniggs.

At the time of the Dissolution, the Barton tithes ('the rectory of Walcot'),
held by the Priory from the Crown, were 'farmed' by Henry Bewshin and
he, followed by his son Peter and later his grandson Thomas, continued
to 'farm' them under those who held *in capite* after the Dissolution. In
1612, Sir George Snigg purchased from the then Crown lessees-in-chief
the tithes of Barton Grange. The sub-tenant at that time (after the
Bewshins) was Robert Chambers (who had also held the lordship of
Walcot, as above), at the annual rent of £10 (which then became payable
to Snigg). Although the tithe of wool and lambs, at 40/- annual rent in
the tenure of Andrew Colthurst (a younger son of Matthew), was
apparently included, a dispute arose as to whether the 40/- should have
been part of the £10 for 'the whole rectory'.[107] The Barton section of Snigg's
Walcot rental, in 1623, states that 'Robert Chambers holdeth for life, and
Humphrey, his brother, the tithes of Barton and some of Walcott' (the
latter possibly 'overland' – see above). Further details appear in the Walcot
Glebe Terrier of 1606 including the fact that Chambers refused to pay the
53/4d due annually to the parson out of the tithes. The Saunders family
succeeded the Sniggs as tenants-in-chief of the rectory of Walcot (the
Barton tithes), the lordship of Walcot, and Barton Farm.

Although the Ham (20 acres), Ambury Mead (6 acres) and Ambury
Orchard (2 acres) in St James's parish are named in the Crown grant of
Barton Grange of 1547, corroborative evidence of Barton status is available
only for the Ham (see above). Of the Barton demesne within the parish
of Walcot, there were in the West Field: Longcroft (meadow, 6 acres,
'beneath the house'); 'the Hayes' (25 acres 'near the house' – see also above);
'the Vineyards' (5 acres – its Field allocation slightly uncertain); 'Sopers'
(in the former detached part of Walcot on Lansdown - see below),
all 'anciently' enclosed; 'Hayes Furlong' (25 acres, near 'the Hayes');
'Kingsmead Furlong' (20 acres, near 'Kingsmead'). The two furlongs
together had probably formed the 'Barton Furlong' of 1501. In the East
Field were: 'East Hayes' (20 acres, 'anciently enclosed') and 'New Tyning'
(7 acres), both sold to Haines in 1639 (see above); 'Prior's Furlong'
(24 acres, 20 of which were sold to Haines in 1638 – see above); 'East
(or Lambridge) Furlong' (20 acres); 'Side Heil' (about 10 acres, but in 1612
given as 30 acres, apparently then including 'East Furlong'); 'Town's End
Land' (about 3 acres, 'lying next to Walcot'); and a ground 'towards
Charlcombe, containing 7 or 8 acres, near Dead Mills Batch' – probably
the ground called 'Catts Cliffe' in the rental of 1623.[108]

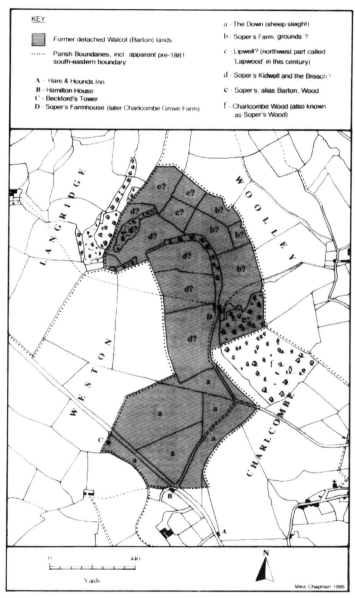

KEY

Former detached Walcot (Barton) lands

····· Parish Boundaries, incl. apparent pre-1881 south-eastern boundary

A - Hare & Hounds Inn
B - Hamilton House
C - Beckford's Tower
D - Soper's Farmhouse (later Charlcombe Grove Farm)

a - The Down (sheep sleight)
b - Soper's Farm grounds ?
c - Lipwell? (northwest part called 'Lapwood' in this century)
d - Soper's Kidwell and the Breach ?
e - Soper's, alias Barton, Wood
f - Charlcombe Wood (also known as Soper's Wood)

Mike Chapman 1995

3. The former detached part of the parish of Walcot (until 1881), at the south-eastern end of Lansdown.

The former detached part of Walcot (originally sheep down, plus largely wooded slopes) was at the south-eastern end of Lansdown, surrounded by Charlcombe, Woolley, Langridge and Weston (see fig. 3). Although unfortunately not included on Thorpe's *Plan of Walcot*, 1740 (the earliest available) nor on the Walcot Tithe Map (presumably because all its 195 acres, as former Priory demesne, were tithe free), tithe maps of the surrounding parishes naturally reveal its former limits. The area was transferred to the parish of Charlcombe in 1881, the resulting boundary changes being confirmed in 1883.[109]

The Tithe Apportionment lists Soapers (sic) Farm, 43 acres; Soapers Kitwell, alias Kidwell and the Breach, 60 acres; Soapers, alias Barton Wood, 12 acres; Lipwell, 20 acres; as well as 60 acres called 'the Down' (on the site of the present Ministry of Defence Ensleigh offices).

In manorial works of 'Berton', c.1467/8-82, are included 'Lypwelle woode, 25 acres; Myddill woode, 8 acres; Cybbill woode, 8 acres'. The last ('Kitwell'/'Kidwell' in the Apportionment) became 'Kybwelle, alias Kipwelle woode ['in the north part'] and the Breache ['south part'] of 8 acres', when obtained as 'concealed land' in a Crown grant of 17 March 1585 (probably because omitted in error from the Crown grant of 1547), although later restored to Barton Grange. From the seventeenth century, as 'Sopers Kibwell and the Breach', its area (presumably including other ground and consisting then of three pastures) is given as '60 acres'. In 1501, 10 acres altogether of pasture 'in le Sopers within the demesne of barton' were leased to a Woolley inhabitant. Both 'Sopers' and 'Lipwell wood' were among lands particularly named in the Barton Grange lease to Henry Bewshin in 1529. The Crown grant of Barton Grange of 1547 included 'Sopers', 'Lipwelles Woode', 'Mydlewoode', and 'portion of pasture of "lez Lawncedown" '. The last (sheep sleight for the Barton Eweflock) was 'le downe ... called Lansdown ... next to a certain farm called Sopers', when sold to Haines (as above) in 1639. The rentals of 1623-41 show '2 acres of wood at Sopers' were held by the Walcot 'virgate' tenant. The name 'Sopers' probably arose because 'the house of Thomas le Sopare' stood in that area in 1296.[110]

Identification of grounds is difficult, as 'Sopers Wood' is the only surviving name, and even that is not in the former Walcot part but where the adjacent Charlcombe Wood (also locally called Sopers Wood) was shown on the Charlcombe Tithe Map. Furthermore, the Tithe Assessment acreage of the detached Walcot area (apart from 'the Down') exceeds the true acreage, and seventeenth-century estimates, by over 20 acres. To add to the confusion, between the 1884 and 1903 OS surveys, 'Sopers Farm' was renamed 'Charlcombe Grove farm', while 'Sopers Wood', beside it, became (incorrectly, but understandably) 'Charlcombe Wood' and vice versa.[111] An octogenarian, life-long, local resident has identified a ground he knows as 'Lapwood' – possibly a corruption of 'Lipwell'.

As already shown, none of the Lyncombe and Widcombe properties (whose subsequent ownership is briefly outlined above) was conveyed by Colthurst to Snigg in 1591. Particularly excepted were 'the pasture of ten bullocks ['in summer' as later evidence shows] now used by the occupier ... of Barton Farm in a certain ground called the Lawn and the ground and wood called Prior's Park and the Coniger [or warren] in Widcombe' and ' the winter pasture and common ... and the wintering ... of the said three hundred and three score sheep [the Barton Eweflock] in Broadmead and Broadcroft, now used by the said farmer ... and now or sometime parcel or belonging to the said farm'. Other pastures in Lyncombe and Widcombe provided summer and (including 'the Lawn') autumn or winter pastures for the Hogg Flock (of Lyncombe) of 322 sheep (see figs. 4 and 5). Despite their inclusion in the Crown grant of 1547, and subsequent conveyance in 1548, the Hogg Flock and their pastures seem not to have belonged to Barton Grange, but to the manor of Lyncombe, although, as with some flocks of other manors, separately leased, even before the Dissolution.[112]

In 1304, Edward I granted Bath Priory ' a yearly fair at their manor of Lyncombe, Somerset, on the vigil and feast of the Invention of the Cross' (3 May) and a 'yearly fair at their manor of La Berton by Bath on the vigil and feast of St Lawrence the Martyr' (10 August). However, the contemporary entry of this grant in the Cartularium Prioratus de Bath is headed (here translated) 'Concerning the fairs of Lyncombe and Lansdown'.[113] Lyncombe Fair was held on the present Bear Flat, above the ancient chapel and hospital of St Cross and St Mary Magdalen, the St Cross dedication presumably accounting for the date of the fair. The Lansdown fair was held opposite the ancient chapel of St Lawrence (near the present *Blathwayt Arms*) on that saint's feast day. In 1335, Edward III granted the Priory an extension of the fair 'at their manor of La Berton by Bath'. This grant also appears in the Cartularium under the heading 'Concerning the fair of Lansdown'.[114]

The fourteenth-century Cartularium evidence clearly suggests that the Barton included that northern part of Lansdown containing St Lawrence's chapel (subsequently incorporated in the present Chapel Farmhouse) and its associated Lansdown Manor Farm lands, lying partly on the plateau, partly below it, as pockets of Weston parish 'in the fields of Langridge'.

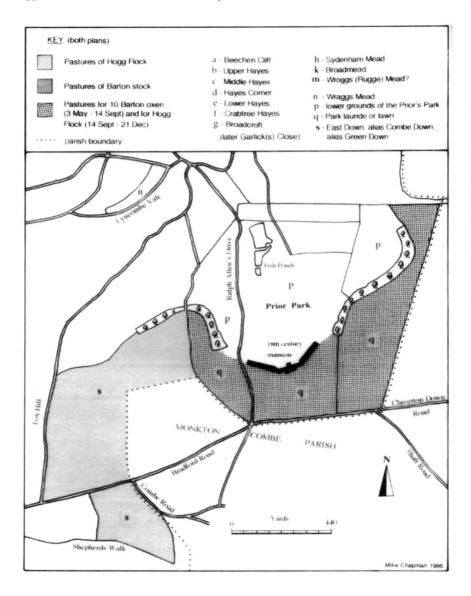

KEY (both plans)

- Pastures of Hogg Flock
- Pastures of Barton stock
- Pastures for 10 Barton oxen (3 May - 14 Sept) and for Hogg Flock (14 Sept - 21 Dec)
- ····· parish boundary

a - Beechen Cliff
b - Upper Hayes
c - Middle Hayes
d - Hayes Corner
e - Lower Hayes
f - Crabtree Hayes
g - Broadcroft
    (later Garlick(s) Close)

h - Sydenham Mead
k - Broadmead
m - Wroggs (Rugge) Mead?

n - Wraggs Mead
p - lower grounds of the Prior's Park
q - Park launde or lawn

s - East Down, alias Combe Down, alias Green Down

Mike Chapman 1995

4 and 5 (opposite). The south-eastern and north-western parts, respectively, of the Manor of Lyncombe (in the former parish of Lyncombe and Widcombe). The key to both maps is shown on fig.4.

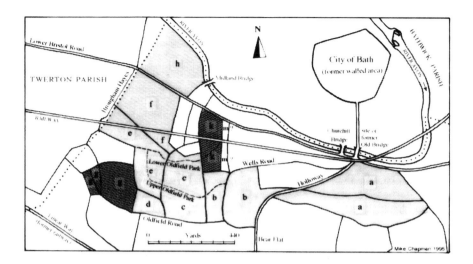

Significantly, later evidence shows that these lands (and some pertaining to the Manor of Weston on the plateau – surprisingly treated as part of the Manor of Lansdown in the Tithe Apportionment) were 'within the parish of Weston and the tithing of Walcot', and that Lansdown Manor was taxed, not with Weston, but with Walcot parish.[115]

Although the detached part of Walcot at the south-eastern end of Lansdown (see above) was invariably shown as part of Barton Grange (which was within both parish and tithing of Walcot), a Priory MS of manorial works, c.1467/8-82,[116] treats the Lansdown Manor Farm lands (by listing them under 'Launcesdon') separately from the Barton Grange lands (listed under 'Berton'). In Ministers' Accounts of 1539, also, the 'Farm of the manor of Launcedon' (listed below 'Weston cum Launcedon, parcell de Weston') and 'Barton Grange and Rectory' are separately treated. Perhaps the distinctive treatment had developed as a matter of administrative convenience. The evidence is somewhat confusing.

The Manors of Weston and Lansdown were held by Bath Priory (under the Crown) until the Dissolution, when they became the subject of various Crown grants and passed through other hands. In the 1570s, Thomas Kerry, a clerk of the privy seal, obtained Weston Manor, subject to a pre-Dissolution lease, and Lansdown Manor (obtaining a further Crown lease of it in 1602) on which he was allowed two fairs, including the traditional St Lawrence's Fair.[117] He was also granted the Lansdown Sheephouse, the Eweflock of 360 sheep, with 'a parcel of le downe', and their pastures,

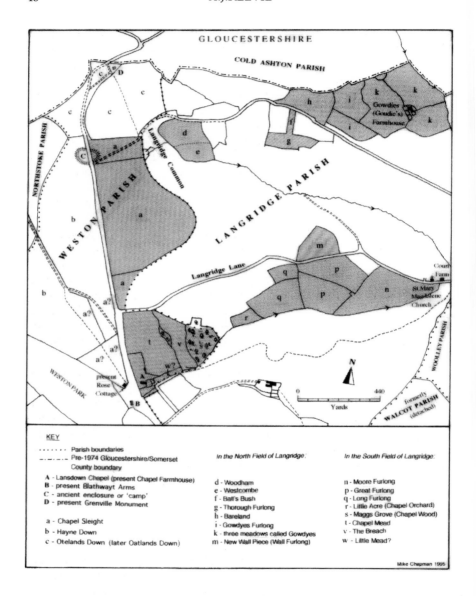

KEY

- ...... Parish boundaries
- -·-·-·- Pre-1974 Gloucestershire/Somerset
  County boundary

- A - Lansdown Chapel (present Chapel Farmhouse)
- B - present Blathwayt Arms
- C - ancient enclosure or 'camp'
- D - present Grenville Monument

- a - Chapel Sleight
- b - Hayne Down
- c - Otelands Down (later Oatlands Down)

In the North Field of Langridge:

- d - Woodham
- e - Westcombe
- f - Ball's Bush
- g - Thorough Furlong
- h - Bareland
- i - Gowdyes Furlong
- k - three meadows called Gowdyes
- m - New Wall Piece (Wall Furlong)

In the South Field of Langridge:

- n - Moore Furlong
- p - Great Furlong
- q - Long Furlong
- r - Little Acre (Chapel Orchard)
- s - Maggs Grove (Chapel Wood)
- t - Chapel Mead
- v - The Breach
- w - Little Mead?

Mike Chapman 1995

6. Lands of the Manor of Lansdown (at the northern extremity of Lansdown and in the fields of Langridge, all being 'in the parish of Weston and the tithing of Walcot').

etc., 'in Langridge and elsewhere'.[118] Kerry also appears to have acquired Bathforum hundred, for, with Weston and Lansdown, it descended through his heirs, including, from 1612, his son-in-law John Winchcombe and two more generations of that name, the recusancy of one resulting in lengthy sequestration (1645-56) of the property. Bathforum hundred and Weston Manor together subsequently passed through other hands, eventually to the Oliver family (as above). Lansdown Manor and certain former Manor of Weston lands on Lansdown passed, during the 1660s, to the occupier, John Sheppard, and he gradually sold his property, much of it in 1701 to William Blathwayt, Secretary of State for War, whose family still possessed it at the time of the Tithe Apportionment.[119]

A Crown grant of 1585 includes Tithes of the Farm of Lansdown 'in the parishes of Weston and Langridge, pertaining to the Free chapel of St Lawrence', in the tenure of the Weston vicar; and the 'ruinous' St Lawrence's Chapel (a royal free chapel), lying in the farm lands of Lansdown, with all tithes and profits issuing out of the chapel, in the tenure of the farmer. The latter (chapel) tithes (probably largely emanating from the former 'Chapel Sleight' on which the chapel stood) passed with the farm, a fact of which the Weston vestry seemed unaware, for the Glebe Terrier of 1606 states that although the farmer paid tithes to the vicar on all other Lansdown farm lands, 'wee knowe not by what righte he detayneth the tithes of that sheepe slaite'.[120]

By 1600, confusion concerning boundaries and ownership of certain Lansdown lands (notably 'Hayne Down' and 'Otelands') led to law-suits. By 1701, the Manor of Lansdown contained certain former Manor of Weston Lansdown lands, including 'Hayne Down'.[121] There are many peculiarities and difficulties concerning the northern part of Lansdown, which have not so far been satisfactorily resolved. Detailed discussion of them has been omitted from the present article.

Conclusion

It has been possible to identify most of the lands of Barton Grange (containing arable, woodland, and both highland and lowland pastures, enabling seasonal movement of the sheep flock) which clearly covered a wide variety of terrain, rising from river-level to well over 700 feet. They were distributed over an extensive area of Walcot (including the former detached part at the south-eastern end of Lansdown), with some meadow and pasture land within the city limits and in Lyncombe. Barton Grange itself with most of its demesne was contained in Walcot, as was also the land allocated to its workforce, who were the inhabitants of this external parish. Although outside the city, the Barton was obviously integral to it, and Bath citizens were able to maintain traditional rights of common upon its demesne in Walcot, both before and after the Dissolution, no matter who held the Barton at fee farm from the king. It has become clear that, in the early days, the holder of the Barton had jurisdiction over the whole hundred of Bath. Thus, by granting the Barton to the ecclesiastical head of the Bath monastic church, whether bishop or prior, successive medieval monarchs continued, until the Dissolution, to honour the purpose of the seventh-century grant of the hundred. At the same time, they maintained the royal connection, by endowing a royal dependant, sometimes their queen, with the fee farm rent payable for the Barton.

The evidence that the most northerly part of Lansdown (the Manor of Lansdown) with its chapel was also within the tithing of Walcot and the Manor of Barton, despite its subsequent separate treatment from Barton Grange, raises many fundamental questions concerning that most dominant and historic hill of Lansdown, and its earlier importance to Bath and its locality, but detailed discussion of this somewhat separate issue would seem inappropriate in the present article. Although it is hoped that the outline study will have thrown more light on the hitherto comparatively little-known subject of the Bath Barton, and contributed to a clearer understanding of its extent, tenure, farming system, and connection with city and hundred, certain aspects remain enigmatic (particularly concerning the Manor of Lansdown) and await further research and debate.

Notes

1   Rev. R.W. Eyton, *Domesday Studies and Somerset Gheld Inquest*, Vol. 1 (1880), pp.49-50, 74 & 106;   C. & F. Thorn eds., *Domesday Book*, No. 8, Somerset (Chichester, 1980), pp.1, 30-31. The hide was an area considered adequate to support one free family and dependants – although varying in extent, normally 120 acres.

2   E. Green ed., 'A Bath Poll Tax of 2 Richard II', *Bath Field Club*, Vol.VI (1889), pp.300-9.

3   J. Wood, *Essay Towards a Description of Bath* (1749, 1765 edition), p.252; Bath Record Office (BRO), Charter 22; P.R. James, bound typescript transcripts, Charters and Documents of Bath (James, Bath Documents) (1942), Part I, No. 22.

4   W. Illingworth ed., *Rotuli Hundredorum* (*Rot Hund*), Vol. II (HMSO, 1818), p.138.

5   Thorn & Thorn, p.370, App.1.

6   B.W.Dobbie, *An English Rural Community: Batheaston with St Catherine* (Bath, 1969), p.17 & App.4 – showing that at Domesday St Catherine was included with the Abbey manor of Batheaston.

7   W. Hunt ed., *Two Chartularies of the Priory of St Peter at Bath* (*Two Chartularies*), Somerset Record Society (SRS), Vol. VII (1893), i, No. 7; see also H.P.R. Finberg ed., *Early Charters of Wessex* (Leicester, 1964), No. 335, correcting the date to 675.

8   M. Sharp, *Accounts of the Constables of Bristol Castle,* Bristol Record Society, Vol.XXIV (1982), Intro.liii, lviii & lix; H.P.R. Finberg, *Gloucestershire Studies* (Leicester, 1957), pp.14-16, 55 & note.

9   Finberg (1957), pp.14-16.

10   M. Aston, 'The Bath Region from Late Prehistory to the Middle Ages', *Bath History* (1986), pp.73-8.

11   *Two Chartularies*, i, Nos. 37, 38, 40 & 43.

12   *Ibid*, No. 56; *ibid*, No. 74; Historical MSS Commission, *Calendar of MSS of Dean & Chapter of Wells*, Vol. 1 (HMSO, 1907), pp.438-9.

13   *Two Chartularies,* i, No. 61.

14   *Ibid*, ii, No. 42.

15   D.M. Stenton ed., *Pipe Roll Society* (Stenton, *PRS*), New series (NS), Vol.VIII (1931), p.139, Roll 43, Rot 9, m 1 – PRO E372.

16   Helen Cam, *The Hundred and the Hundred Rolls* (1930, 1963 edition), p.145.

17   D.M.M. Shorrocks ed., 'Walker-Heneage Deeds' in *Medieval Deeds of Bath and District,* SRS, Vol. LXXIII (1974), ii, 94/409.

18   *Two Chartularies*, Intro. l-liii.

19   Stenton, *PRS*, NS, Vol. VI (1929), p.46, 7 Rich I, Roll 41, Rot 4d, m 2.

20   *Rot Hund*, Vol. II, p.132.

21   Rev. R. Warner, *History of Bath* (1801), Appendix XXVIII from Augmentations Office, Cart S. 68.

22   *Rot Hund,* Vol. II, p.132; see also Pipe Roll for Michaelmas, 1204, 6 John, Roll 14, Rot 14d, m 1 in Stenton, *PRS*, NS, Vol. XVIII (1940), p.184.

23   *Rot Hund*, Vol. II, p.133.

24   E. Green ed., *Feet of Fines of the County of Somerset,* SRS, Vol. VI (1892), No. 101.

25   'County Rate, 1742' and 'Census, 1841' in F.H. Dickinson ed., *Kirby's Quest etc.*, SRS, Vol. III (1889), pp.285-6 and 312.

26   *Two Chartularies*, ii, Nos. 361 and 364; Shorrocks, SRS, Vol. LXXIII (1974), ii, Nos. 89 and 128.

27   B.R. Kemp ed., 'Medieval Deeds of St John's Hospital, Bath' in *Medieval Deeds of Bath and District*, SRS, Vol.LXXIII (1974), i, No. 47.

28   Information from *Manorial Documents Register,* Royal Commission on Historical Manuscripts.

29   Estate Documents, Nos. 1178, 1181 and 1186.

30   BRO, Corporation Deeds, Bundle VI, Nos. 71-2 (original documents); Rev. C.W. Shickle, *Ancient Deeds of Bath Corporation* (Bath, 1921), Bundle VI,

Nos. 71-2 (transcripts and translation).

31   Public Record Office (PRO), Charter Rolls, 20, Henry III, C53/29, m 6.
     (Phrase omitted in published Calendar).

32   *Calendar of Patent Rolls* , 1 Ed. I (HMSO, 1924-9), p.12, m 15; p.30, m 4.

33   *Two Chartularies*, Nos. 609 and 610; *Calendar of Charter Rolls*, 3 Edward I,
     Vol. II (HMSO, 1906), p.192, No. 5, m 4; *Calendar of Close Rolls*, 1272-9,
     3 Edward I, p.245, m 6d.

34   Rev Chancellor T. Scott Holmes, 'Ecclesiastical History' in W. Page ed.,
     Victoria County History of Somerset, Vol. II (1911), pp.90-1.

35   *Two Chartularies*,ii, No. 666.

36   *Calendar of Patent Rolls*, 1272-81 (HMSO, 1901), 3 Edward I, p.91, m 22 and
     p.94, m 20.

37   *Ibid*, 1299 (1895), 27 Edward I, p.452, m 4.

38   *Calendar of Charter Rolls*, Vol. III (1908), p.416, m 6; *Calendar of Inquisitions
     Post Mortem*, Vol. XIX, 1405-13 (HMSO, 1992), No. 865.

39   Excavations, Bath Archaeological Trust, 1989-91. Preliminary Reports, *Bath
     Museums Service News*, Autumn 1989, Spring 1990 and *Bath Archaeology*,
     News Sheet 6; Bath Archaeological Trust, Finds record, Bronze Age axe,
     Pera Place, Walcot.

40   A. Mawer & F.M. Stenton, *Place Names of Worcestershire* (Cambridge, 1927),
     p.221; J. Haslam, 'Saxon Bath' in J. Haslam ed., *Anglo-Saxon Towns*
     (Chichester, 1984), note 1, p.356.

41   *Two Chartularies*, ii, No. 61.

42   B. Cunliffe, *Roman Bath* (Reports of Research Committee of the Society of
     Antiquaries of London, No. XXIV, 1969), pp.211-2 and 214-5; F.W. Weaver,
     Wells Wills (1890), pp.178-9; F. Bond, *Dedications and Patron Saints of English
     Churches* (Oxford, 1914), p.60.

43   Dickinson, SRS, Vol. III (1889), p.83.

44   Somerset Record office (SRO), Walcot rentals, 1501 – DD/X/HY 1; and
     c.1560/1-1641 – DD/BR/Sb2 N/68.

45   J. Manco, 'Henry Savile's Map of Bath', *Proceedings of Somerset Archaeological
     & Natural History Society (PSANHS)*, Vol. 136 (1992), p.132 & Plate 2;
     Bath Library, J. Gilmore, *Map of Bath*, 1694.

46   Warner (1801), p.187; BRO, Rivers Estate, sale particulars (1856), Lots 147-
     155, pp.5-6 & plate 5.

47   SRO, indenture, 1768 – DD/BR/PY/125 C/492; Bath Library, collection
     of Bath photographs, Barton House, c.1849.

48   *Rot Hund*, Vol. II, p.138.

49   *Two Chartularies*, ii, No. 744.

50   H.P.R. Finberg, *Tavistock Abbey*, Cambridge Studies Vol. II (Cambridge,
     1951), pp.239-40; H.S. Bennett, *Life on the English Manor*, (Gloucester, 1987
     edition), pp.163ff.

51   *Calendar of Patent Rolls*, Richard II, Vol. I, p.251, m 26d.

52   PRO, C260/91, No. 51 – reference by courtesy of Mrs. J. Manco.

53   Walcot rental, 1501 – *op. cit.*

54   Bath Library, P. R. James, 'The Incorporation of the City of Bath',
     unpublished University of London thesis, undated, post-1940, pp.201-2.

55 SRO, DD/BR/Sb2 N/68, Item 3, Walcot rental, c.1600.

56 *Ibid*, Walcot rentals, 1623-41.

57 C.C. Dyer, 'Farming Practices and Techniques', in E. Miller ed., *Agrarian History of England and Wales*, Vol.III, 1348-1500 (Cambridge, 1991), p.79.

58 Walcot rental, 1501 – *op.cit.*; and Walcot rentals, 1623-41 – *op. cit.*

59 PRO, SC2/198, Nos. 27-40.

60 BRO, Account Book of the Prior of Bath, 20 Henry VIII, fo.157 – MS copy in Freemen's Estate, Box 1, No. 53.

61 BRO, original document, Freemen's Estate, Box 1, No. 25.

62 BRO, original document, Acc. 28, No. 31.

63 *Two Chartularies*, No. 709.

64 Dyer (1991), p.222; SRO, Jacobean Glebe Terriers of parishes in Bathforum hundred.

65 BRO, Freemen's Estate, Box 1, No. 43, MS, c.1612, prepared for law-suit.

66 BRO, T. Thorpe, *Plan of the Parish of Walcot*, 1740.

67 BRO, Freemen's Estate, Box 1, No. 43, MS, c.1612.

68 Langridge Glebe Terrier, 1606, shows Hospital land at Beacon Hill in East Field (No. 91 on Thorpe's *Plan*, 1740, & schedule) – SRO, D/D/Rg 9; conveyance of 29 April 1699, privately held, of lands sold to W. Hooper in West Field (Nos. 79, 86 &87 on Thorpe's *Plan*, 1740), transcribed, Rev. C.W. Shickle (1900), MS notebook No. 20, p.23 – Bath Library, A32.1123.

69 Shickle (1900), p.50, transcription of indenture of 1737, in private collection.

70 *Two Chartularies*, No. 709; James, thesis, p.249, quoting PRO, E/318/1685, m 24, Aug. Off. Ptics. for Grants. Other spellings of Bewshin include Bewsham, Bewshine, Bewshyne and Bewchyn.

71 *Ibid*; see also PRO, SC6, Roll 3144, Ministers' Accounts, 1539; and SRO, T/PH/VCH6, Roll 3144, microfilm copy.

72 BRO, MS copy of Memo from Account Book of the Prior of Bath, 7 Henry VIII, fo.115, in Freemen's Estate, Box 1, No. 53.

73 Ministers' Accounts, 1539 – *op. cit.*; see also James, thesis, p.201.

74 PRO, E313, Patent Rolls, 16 July 1585, 27 Elizabeth I, Pt. iv, C66/1257, m 45; see also James, thesis, p.202.

75 *Valor Ecclesiasticus* of 1535.

76 *Calendar of State Papers, Domestic & Foreign*, Vol. XVI (HMSO, 1898), Pt.I, item 779 (7) – PS Pat p.6, mm 33-6.

77 James, thesis, p.263, quoting AO Parl Surveys, E317/22, 4.

78 Rev. J. Collinson, *The History and Antiquities of the County of Somerset*, Vol. 1 (Bath, 1791), p.98; BRO, Abstract of Title, 1611-1751 – Freemen's Estate, Box 1, No. 99 misc.

79 Dickinson (1889), p.312; Bath Library, Silverthorne's *Bath Directory*, 1841, p.210.

80 BRO, Court-Book, 1801-69.

81 *Calendar of Patent Rolls*, 1 Edward VI, Vol. 1 (HMSO, 1924), pp.194-5, m 13.

82 BRO, Acc. 28, No. 8.

83 *Calendar of State Papers*, Henry VIII, Vol. XVIII (HMSO, 1901), item 346, (40) Pt. II – Pat, p.7, m 6.

84 William Sherston was grandfather of the well-known William Prynne (born 1600); BRO, Acc. 28, No. 8. Other spellings of Snigg include Snigge and Snygge.

85   BRO, E. Lucas, undated, typescript transcript, Egerton charter 5824,
      Kingston Estate Papers at Nottingham.
86   BRO, Ralph Allen Estate Papers, Boxes 1 (no. 1) & 2.
87   BRO, deed, Acc. 28, No. 8.
88   BRO, Acc. 28, No. 32.
89   *Ibid*, Nos. 37 & 40, original documents.
90   Thorpe's *Plan* & schedule.
91   BRO, Corporation documents, Bundle 6, No. 73.
92   BRO, Acc. 28, No. 8.
93   British Library, Abstract of Title, Egerton charter 3647, f.132 – copy transcript
      kindly provided by Miss E. Holland.
94   SRO, DD/BR/Sb2 N/68.
95   SRO, D/D/Rg 15.
96   Egerton charter 3647, *op. cit.*, f.109.
97   SRO, lease of 1656 – DD/BR/Sb3 N/68.
98   *Ibid.*
99   SRO, deed – DD/X/FRC 1 C/71.
100   BRO, Deed Packet 3086.
101   Bath Library, MS 1699, Walcot Estate Papers.
102   Wood (1765), pp.240-3. Wood purchased parts of it for his building schemes.
103   Rev. R.G. Bartelot, 'New Light on Bath Abbey and Priory', *PSANHS*, Bath
      Branch (1939-47), p.180.
104   SRO, Walcot rentals and survey, 1623-41 – DD/BR/Sb2 N/68.
105   J. Youings, 'The Church', in J. Thirsk ed., *Agrarian History of England and
      Wales*, Vol. IV, 1500-1640 (Cambridge, 1967), pp.311-2.
106   Calendar of Patent Rolls, Elizabeth I, Vol. VI, p.448, C66/1127, Pt. V, No. 2823,
      Pt. viii, sub-sections 1 & 8, mm 1-7; BRO, P.R. James (1942), *op. cit.*, Part II,
      note to No. 43; Walcot rentals and survey, 1623-41.
107   'Farm of the Rectory' amounting to £10 in Ministers' Accounts, 1539 – *op. cit.*;
      BRO, deed, Acc. 28, No. 8; Walcot rental, 1623; James, thesis, p.204.
108   Information from various sources, including Walcot rentals, 1623-41, giving
      names and acreages of most grounds; and BRO, Freemen's Estate, Box 1,
      Nos. 19-22, descriptions in depositions, law-suit, 1612.
109   PRO, OS map 29/288 & description 1526/9145 & 9147.
110   SRO, DD/X/HY 1; SRO, DD/SE 28, Box 4; Barton sections, Walcot rentals,
      1623-41, *op. cit.*; British Library, Cartularium Prioratus de Bath, Egerton
      MS 3316, f.55d; Bath Library, P.R. James, photostat copy and MS transcript
      of Cartularium (1952).
111   1:2,500 OS map, Somerset VIII, 9 & 13 (1887); cf. 1884 with 1903 and
      subsequent OS maps.
112   The manor was 'Lincumba' (Lyncombe) at Domesday and later, but in the
      seventeenth century it was known as 'the manor of Lyncombe and Widcombe'.
      A lease of 18 May 1614 (in SRO, DD/SE 28, Box 4) refers to 'Widcombe alias
      Woodcombe in the tithing of Lyncombe'; 'lawn' or 'laund' is 'a glade or open
      space among woods or in a park' (OED); British Library, Harleian MS 3970, fo.30
      (Priory leases).
113   *Calendar of Charter Rolls*, 1300-1326, Vol. III (HMSO, London, 1908), p.47,

m 1; Cartularium Prioratus de Bath, *op. cit.*, f.26.

114   Rev. W. Stokes Shaw, 'Notes on the Chapel and Hospital of St Mary
       Magdalene', *Bath Field Club*, Vol. II (1869), p.106; *Calendar of Charter Rolls,
       1327-41*, Vol. IV (1912), p.341, m 9; *Cartularium, op. cit.*, f.48d; '28/4d –
       issues of the fairs of Lyncombe and Launcedon', sole item under 'Hundred
       of Berton – issues of the hundred' in Ministers' Accounts, 1539, *op. cit.*

115   Crown grant of 17 March 1585 – SRO, DD/SE 28, Box 4; also in *Draft Patent
       Rolls*, List & Index Society, Vol. 241 (1990), pp.9-11, 27 Elizabeth I, Pt. 1,
       C66/1254, m 39; SRO, Tithe Maps of Weston and Langridge; Gloucestershire
       Record Office (GRO), 'Articles of Agreement', 1700 in D/1799, T64;
       see also Wood (1765), p.128 and Collinson (1791), Vol. 1, p.159; Bath
       Library, Rev. C. W. Shickle (sometime rector of Langridge), MS notebook on
       Langridge and neighbourhood (c.1895) – A50.345 re Lansdown Manor tax.

116   SRO, DD/X/HY 1.

117   *Calendar of Patent Rolls*, Elizabeth I (HMSO, 1939 ff), Vol. V, No. 2522
       (16 July 1572), mm 12-15; a large grain rent of wheat, barley and oats was
       'due yearly from the farmer of the Manor of Weston and lands of Launcedowne'
       – *ibid*; GRO, D/1799, T62 – conveyance from Crown lessee (11 June 1573);
       also Crown patent (5 July 1602); *Calendar of Patent Rolls*, Elizabeth I, Vol. VII,
       Pt. IV, C66/1140 (13 April 1576), No. 477, m 22.

118   *Calendar of Patent Rolls*, Elizabeth I, Vol. VII, Pt. II, C66/1165, No. 2690
       (30 June 1578), mm 34-5. The Eweflock wintered in Corston, Stanton Prior
       and Priston; see M. Costen, 'Stantonbury and District', *Bristol and Avon
       Archaeology*, Vol. II (1983), p.33, quoting a survey of 1530 in SRO, DD/BR/c 1402.

119   BRO, Abstracts of Title, No. 26; M.A.E. Green ed., *Calendar of the Proceedings
       of the Committee for Compounding, 1643-60* (HMSO, London, 1889-92),
       Pt. I, p.725; Pt. III, p.2363; Pt. V, pp.3302-3; BRO, Abstracts of Title, No. 26;
       GRO, D/1799, T64-65 (various conveyances); *ibid*, T67.

120   Crown grant of 15 March 1585 – *op. cit.*; GRO, D/1799, T67 – conveyance
       of 25 March 1701; SRO, D/D/wae/3/1/1 (Weston Glebe Terrier).

121   PRO, E112, Exchequer Bills & Answers, Som 203, Easter, 7 James I (1609);
       1701 conveyance, *op. cit.* ; see also Tithe Apportionment.

Acknowledgements

The writer wishes to express his grateful thanks to Joe Bettey, Peter Davenport and Jean Manco for their kindness in perusing his preparatory work upon which he has based the present article, and for providing him with most valuable advice and encouragement; to Elizabeth Holland, Marta Inskip, Trevor Fawcett and other frequenters of Bath Record Office for their readiness to share with him information from their own spheres of interest; to the staff of the Bath, Gloucestershire, Somerset and Public Record Offices, but especially of Bath and of Bath Reference Library for their patient helpfulness in many enquiries; and to Mike Chapman for his skilful draughtmanship.

LIFE AND LITIGATION IN BATH AND ITS ENVIRONS IN THE SIXTEENTH CENTURY

J.H.Bettey

A remarkable feature of English local communities during the sixteenth and seventeenth centuries was the readiness with which they resorted to litigation and the number of expensive legal suits over comparatively trivial matters which were brought before the central courts of equity in London. This willingness of all classes to sue before the royal courts brought great wealth to lawyers and must frequently have cost more in legal fees than the dispute was worth; for historians, the voluminous records of the courts provide a rich harvest of evidence concerning all sorts of local issues and throw light on many aspects of local society which would otherwise remain hidden. The various central courts such as Chancery, Exchequer, Star Chamber and Requests all used the same method of following a complaint from a plaintiff by the appointment of commissioners to collect evidence in the form of depositions from local witnesses, and since the testimony was written down at length and in English by long-suffering clerks, much incidental information can be found in the statements beyond the declarations about the case at issue. A search through some of the relevant court records in the Public Record Office reveals a variety of evidence about Bath and its neighbourhood in the mid-sixteenth century, and in particular shows the upheavals in land ownership caused by the suppression of the religious houses and the dispersal of their estates. With so much former ecclesiastical property, Bath and district was inevitably greatly affected, and the long-running disputes to which the land transfers gave rise provide evidence about the landscape, tenure, farming and trade. They show the importance of agriculture and the woollen-cloth trade in the economy of Bath, the crucial role of the great sheep flocks with their carefully managed grazing land on Lansdown, the continuing use of the baths, and above all, the ruthless determination of the new class of entrepreneurs to acquire and hold as much of the newly-released lands as possible.

An early dispute involved the hospital of St Mary Magdalen in the Holloway which consisted of a chapel with an attached house for lepers,

supported by lands worth £4 15s 8d per annum.[1] Like the hospital of St
John in Bath, it was administered by the Prior of Bath Abbey, and in 1536
Simon Shepparde, clerk, was appointed as master.[2] After the suppression
of the abbey in 1539, Simon Shepparde instigated two suits before the
Court of Requests complaining that a former monk from the abbey, John
Bekynton alias Romsey, had removed many of the books and ornaments
from the hospital chapel and had usurped Shepparde's position as master,
granting leases of the property and receiving the profits. Bekynton had
been granted an annual pension of £6 13s 4d on the suppression of the
abbey, and had gone to the University of Oxford.[3] In his reply to
Shepparde's allegations, he stated that while he was a monk at Bath he
had been ordered by the Prior, William Holway, to celebrate mass at
the Hospital chapel three or more times a week, but that each time he
took with him a chalice 'wherewith to celebrate masse there and found
all other ornaments and thyngs belonging unto the said chapell of St
Mary Magdalen and pore lazar people in a house adjonant to the same'.[4]
Bekynton went on to deny Shepparde's right to the mastership, and
alleged that the lead from the chapel roof had been stolen by Shepparde
and replaced with tiles. In defence of his title to the hospital Shepparde
brought a case before the Court of Chancery compelling one of the
tenants, Walter Cree, to produce the hospital deeds and other evidences.[5]
Shepparde retained the mastership until 1570, and a list of the goods of
the chapel which were confiscated under Edward VI in 1552 reveals a
rich stock of plate and vestments, including two silver chalices, crosses,
candlesticks, a censer, pyx, pax, bells, several statues and other precious
goods. It also shows that the hospital possessed a flock of 90 sheep, six
oxen and four other beasts.[6] Since the hospital possessed two chalices of
its own, it is curious that Bekynton should have brought one with him
from the abbey in order to celebrate mass; moreover, the total absence
of any books from the hospital in the 1552 list may give strength to
Shepparde's assertion that Bekynton had taken them with him to Oxford.

Even more informative about lands and property is a long-running series
of disputes about the rights and ownership of the estates of St John's
Hospital. One suit brought before the Court of Chancery in 1538 involved
a tenement within the north gate of Bath and five acres of pasture in the
parish of Walcot which had been leased to Isabell Chancellor, widow,
now deceased.[7] Other land belonging to the hospital included 36 acres of
arable and six acres of meadow in Kingsmead outside the west gate of
Bath, 37 acres of arable in the north field and pasture for 100 sheep on
Lansdown. There was also a barn in Kingsmead together with an ox

shippon and pasture rights for four oxen.[8] With so much valuable
ecclesiastical property coming on to the market either for sale or lease,
there was a frantic struggle for possession by the new men who were
eager to establish their fortunes on the rapidly-rising land values of the
period. Many of the lands of St John's were acquired by William Crouch
of Wellow and Englishcombe whose influence and concerns were to be
found everywhere in Bath. In spite of spending a period in the Fleet prison
in 1540 for having been heard to utter unwise thoughts about the King,
including the suggestion that 'a man for money might buy and sell the
Crown of England', Crouch had sufficiently established his wealth and
reputation by 1547 to be appointed to the lucrative office of receiver of
rents in Somerset for Edward Seymour, Duke of Somerset, who was the
King's uncle.[9] The wealth he acquired enabled Crouch to add to his lands
at Wellow and Englishcombe by the acquisition of former monastic
property at Newton St Loe and Hinton Charterhouse, and by the purchase
in 1553 of the manor of Bathampton (Hampton).[10] In 1554 he was elected
to Parliament as one of the members for Bath. William Crouch is a good
example of the new breed of aggressive entrepreneurs who exploited to
the full the opportunities offered by the times, and the numerous disputes
in which he and his son, Walter Crouch, were involved over their newly-
acquired properties provide much evidence about the agricultural land
which almost everywhere still abutted the medieval walls of Bath. In
particular we learn about the large sheep flocks of Walcot, Barton and
Weston, their regular pattern of grazing on Lansdown, and their pastures
at Hayes, Sydenham, Bychyncliffe, Wydcombe and Lyncombe, and the
customary works on the former demesnes of the abbey owed by the
tenants of Walcot and Barton.[11] Much of this property is specified in a
grant to the rising courtier Sir William Herbert in 1547.[12] Other land on
the west side was acquired by the Bewsham or Bewshin family, and a
complex dispute during the 1570s between William and Peter Bewsham,
the sons of Henry Bewsham, and Walter Crouch, reveals further
information about the farming of the lands belonging to 'the brethren
and sisters of the Hospital of St John' in that area, especially details of the
sheep flock and the grazing right on Lansdown where the hospital flock
was by custom driven after the Barton flock from the abbey demesne.[13]

Because long leases of their lands had been granted by the religious
houses in the years before their suppression, possibly in an attempt to
secure influential friends, the disputes over the eventual title to these
lands dragged on throughout the sixteenth century. Court cases during
the reign of Queen Elizabeth concerning the former abbey land at Weston

and Bathford (Ford) provide much evidence concerning farming and topography. The legal suit at Weston was brought by William Aprice whose father, Robert, had obtained a 70-year lease of the manor and sheep flock from the abbey in 1534. It hinged upon the rights to receive the benefits of the sheep fold on the arable land, and the long depositions of more than twenty witnesses taken 'att Weston neare the Citie of Bathe' on 31 December 1588 all refer to the thin soils at Weston which were dependent upon the dung of the sheep fold if satisfactory crops of corn were to be grown. Witnesses stated that 'the growndes and arable lands are become very barren for wante of helpe by pennyng the said Ewe Flocke numbering 540 sheepe which heretofore hath byn the chiefeste maintenance thereof ... the nature of the soile [is] to become barren except yt be from tyme to tyme relieved with Soile and composte of shepe as the Custom of the Countrie ys ...'[14] The sheep flock had customarily been folded upon the fallow arable lands at Weston from the feast of the Annunciation (25 March) until the feast of All Saints (1 November) each year. All the witnesses spoke of the continuing obligation of the tenants at Weston to pay corn rents. These had originated in the food supplied to the monks by their tenants, and were maintained by the new owners of the estates after the dissolution of the abbey. They also laid stress on the poor quality of the corn grown at Weston so that the new landowners refused to accept it as corn rent, and even the poor of Bath would not eat bread made from flour grown at Weston. They stated that this was because of the nature of the land which was 'subjecte unto Tares, Fetches and purse otes, and naturallie doth yelde a thicker hull and less Flower than the grayne [grown] elsewhere'. Not surprisingly in view of the date (1588), several witnesses referred to the costs of 'musters and other warlyke preparations'. The complex dispute over this matter of great importance for the tenant farmers of Weston had still not been settled in 1612, by which time much of the common arable fields were being enclosed, as was a good deal of the grazing land on the lower slopes of Lansdown.[15]

A dispute over the former abbey lands at Bathford occupied the later years of the sixteenth century, and was concerned among other things with the right to a path by which the inhabitants of the hamlet of Warleigh had customarily walked to the parish church at Bathford. The path came through an old orchard and past the manor house 'unto the dore of the Pigeon house there'. It also came through the former common fields where much enclosure had already taken place and it was stated that the 'metes and bounds' of the strips and furlongs had been altered 'by reason they have so long tyme been enjoyed with other lands ... that they cannot now be certainly found out or severed the one from the other'. During the case documents were produced bearing the seal of Bath Abbey with the date 1 June 12 Henry VI (1434), and a lease of the lands to William Button, gentleman, of Alton Priors, Wiltshire, 5 September 29 Henry VIII (1537). Again, the sheep flock for folding on the arable land was an important feature of the manorial economy, and there are references to the sheep grazing land on Bannerdown, Hayes, Rowborough, Goatacre, Monkendown and elsewhere.[16]

Another part of the complex and lengthy dispute concerning the former abbey land at Bathford was tried before the Court of Exchequer between 1605 and 1607. This was initiated by William Ducke and Susan, his wife, who had leased the lands at Bathford from William Button whose family estate also included several manors in Wiltshire. They complained to the Court that John Pearse, who was a tenant at Bathford, had wrongfully occupied 'one messuage and divers tenements, lands, meadowes and pastures'. The Court appointed a commission headed by Sir Edward Hungerford to enquire into the matter and to take evidence from 'the ancientest Tenants of the said Mannor'. The Commissioners ordered that all the 'Terriers, Surveys, Deedes and other evidences concerning the landes in question' should be produced and examined by Sir George Snigge of Bristol, who was one of the Barons of the Exchequer, 'and to be disposed of as he shall see fit'. He advised that since the precise bounds of the lands in dispute were lost, a jury should be appointed to set out new boundaries. In his adjudication he referred to the lands at Barnards Downe, Rowborough, Stocketts Hay, Chesterwell, Monksdowne and elsewhere within the manor. The Survey of the manor which was made in connection with this dispute in 1605 provides a complete picture of it, listing the tenants, their holdings, tenements, gardens and orchards, and the fields and common grazing land of Bathford. Thirty-two copyhold tenants are listed, holding a total of 697 acres, with arable lands in Southfield, Northfield and Eastfield. With 323 acres William Ducke had by far the largest holding, which included two corn mills, a fulling mill, rights of fishing along the Avon, two pigeon houses, and feeding for a flock of 180 sheep. The Survey also included a detailed perambulation of the manor bounds. The long dispute over the lands at Bathford in 1605-7 led to the production of a detailed plan or sketch map of the village (reproduced here by courtesy of Mr. Simon Heneage). This shows houses and buildings, including the church and church house, drawn in elevation and with the names of the tenants; roads and pathways including the path to the church from Warleigh; the site and foundations of the former manor house, Forde

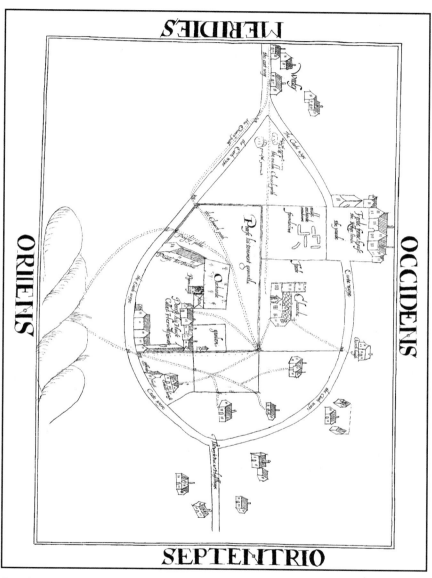

farmhouse, and the complex building called Heriotts Court occupied by John Pearse, together with its large barn, pigeon house, orchard and garden; and the road to Box and Haselbury. The mass of written evidence, together with the map produced because of the dispute at Bathford, is a good example of how informative such legal controversies can be for the local historian.[17]

Earlier in the sixteenth century, the ruthless scramble for monastic land and the lengths to which ambitious and determined men would go to acquire it is shown in a dispute over the manor of Bathwick which came before the Court of Chancery in 1538. This manor had belonged to the nunnery of Wherwell in Hampshire which was suppressed in 1536. Shortly before their dissolution the abbess and nuns had leased Bathwick to Thomas Style at a yearly rent of £17 0s 0d. It had been sub-let to Nicholas Saunders, who complained to the Court that he had been evicted from the lands. Again, the figure of William Crouch appears in the background, for Saunders alleged that Crouch had conspired with one John Cooke, registrar to the Bishop of Winchester, and that together they had 'subtilly and craftily contrived to counterfeit the hand of Richard Pawlett esquire surveyor to the King's Highness of the suppressed landes and of William Kermes one of the auditors of the Court of Augmentations'. With these forged signatures they had sent Saunders a letter addressed from the royal court at Windsor ordering him in the King's name to vacate the property immediately 'without any farder delaye as ye wyll answer thereunto at your Perill'. Saunders claimed that the signatures of Pawlett and Kermes 'were subscribed without their assent or Knowledge' and that he 'being a pore and ympotent man' sought the aid of the Court. In this case his plea was in vain against such wealthy and influential opponents and he was obliged to quit the property at Bathwick which was subsequently leased to Robert Orells.[18]

Several disputes reveal the continuing importance of Bath and district in cloth production, and the wealth derived from woollen cloth is evident from the number of persons described as clothmakers, fullers, tuckers, weavers, tailors and mercers who are found to be investing in parcels of former monastic land around the city. One example is William Chapman, a member of a wealthy family of clothiers in Bath, who rose to prominence in the affairs of the city in the sixteenth century. Their avid desire to acquire land is evident from a complaint made to the Court of Chancery in 1537 by William Felior, a broadloom weaver. Felior stated that he and his wife, Margaret, had the copyhold lease for their lives from Bath Abbey of land in Widcombe called Daweshold 'lying within the parish of Wytcombe for terme of their lyves after the custom of the manor'. He alleged that they had been persuaded to surrender this lease in the manorial court of Widcombe to 'William Chapman of Bath being a Tucker and a great clothmaker', in return for a verbal agreement that Chapman would thereafter provide him with sufficient work for one broad loom. Felior believed that 'he myght gayne more towards his lyving yerely of himselfe and his wyf and children by his said craft as a drawer of woollen cloth' than he could obtain from the land, and therefore agreed to Chapman's suggestion. Now Chapman had refused to perform his part of the bargain and denied that he had ever agreed to provide work for Felior in return for the lease.[19]

John Bysse of Publow was another wealthy clothier who eagerly acquired former monastic land during the 1540s, while his nephew, James Bysse of Stoke St Michael, bought an even larger estate including the Bath Abbey lands at Englishcombe and Chelwood.[20] Likewise in 1544 John Malte, tailor, and his illegitimate daughter, Ethelreda Malte alias Dyngley, were wealthy enough to pay £1,311 0s 2d for the lordship of Kevelston (Kelston) which had been part of the vast estates of the nunnery at Shaftesbury, and to buy the flock of 400 ewes called 'le yowe flocke of Charmerdown' together with their grazing land in St Catherines and Ford (Bathford) formerly part of the possessions of Bath Abbey.[21] Robert Long, mercer, of London paid £783 0s 6d for numerous scattered pieces of monastic land around Bath, including coal mines at Stratton-on-the-Fosse, lands at Chilcompton and Midsomer Norton and 'three messuages in the tenure of James Hogan in Chepestrete, Bath'.[22]

Finally, a feature of life in Bath during the later sixteenth century which emerges from an examination of these disputes over land and property is the increasing power, influence and pretensions of the Corporation of Bath which, in the decades following the suppression of the abbey, assumed control over more and more aspects of life in the city. This can be illustrated from the manner in which the Corporation obtained control of the baths. By a grant of 1550, the management of the baths which had been controlled by the abbey was vested by the Crown into the hands of Humphrey Cotton, physician. The grant stated that 'by long study in the art of physic [he] has founde how to cure and heale any our subjectes or other persons, being deseased of dyvers infirmities, maladies or deseases and kyndes of goute by vertue of the water of our bathes, commonly caulyd the welles or bathes of Bathe Towne'. The grant was for Cotton's life, in return for 4d a day and with the proviso that one bath was to be reserved 'from tyme to tyme for the free use of the poor'.[23]

Soon afterwards, however, Humphrey Cotton is found making a petition to the Court of Requests in which he complained that notwithstanding his grant for life, the mayor of Bath, John Davis, Richard Chapman and Edward Ludwell, with other 'brethren of the Corporation' had forcibly taken the keys of the baths from him, refusing him entry to the baths and reducing him to complete ruin, 'to his undoing and the undoing of his wife and nine children'. He also claimed to have spent large sums and much labour in adapting, cleansing and repairing the baths.[24] The dispute was finally settled after arbitration when it was agreed that Cotton should surrender his claim to the baths to the Corporation in return for a payment of £90.[25] With the baths and other former church property in the hands of a self-confident Corporation the scene was set for the gradual transformation of Bath from a church-dominated, cloth-producing town to the tourist centre and major spa which it was to become.

Notes

1   Public Record Office (PRO), SC6/Henry VIII 3144.
2   *Letters & Papers of Henry VIII*, X, 1536, 777(2).
3   *Ibid*, XIV, Pt. 1, 1539, 1355(121).
4   PRO, REQ2/8/217; REQ2/11/101.
5   PRO, C1/903/30-31.
6   PRO, E117/8/23.
7   PRO, C1/742/554-55.
8   PRO, REQ2/101/59.
9   *Letters & Papers of Henry VIII*, XV, 1540, 689; *Calendar of State Papers (Domestic)*, Edward VI, 1547-53, 575.
10   PRO, E318/1560.
11   *Letters & Papers of Henry VIII*, XVIII, Pt. 1, 346(37); 982(1276).
12   *Calendar of Patent Rolls*, Edward VI, I, 194-5.
13   PRO, REQ2/101/59.
14   PRO, E134/31 Elizabeth Hil. 25.
15   PRO, E134/9 James I East. 5. For other evidence concerning Weston see PRO, REQ2/132/8; C1/899/35-37. For similar disputes over land at North Stoke and Swainswick see PRO, E134/24-25 Eliz. Mich. 6; E134/26-27 Eliz. Mich. 8; C1/815/19.
16   PRO, E178/4446. G.F. Laurence, *Bathford Past and Present* (Bathford, 1985). For property in Bath held by the Button family see PRO, C3/301/9.
17   Somerset Record Office, DD/Whb Box 59/1 Evidence re Bathford land 1605-7; DD/Whb Box 59/2 Plan of Bathford village, c.1605; DD/SK1/1 Survey of Bathford 1605-6.
18   PRO, C1/894/11.
19   PRO, C1/787/28.
20   PRO, E318/198, 220; *Letters & Papers of Henry VIII*, XIX, Pt.1, 1544, 1035(115); *Calendar of Patent Rolls*, Edward VI, V, 1553, 211-13.
21   *Letters & Papers of Henry VIII*, XXI, Pt. 2, 1546-7, 200(33); B.M. Dobbie, *An English Rural Community: Batheaston with St Catherine* (Bath, 1969), p.17.
22   *Letters & Papers of Henry VIII*, XIX, Pt. 2, 1545, 496(57).
23   *Calendar of Patent Rolls*, Edward VI, III, 1550, 309.
24   PRO, REQ2/20/42.
25   A.J. King & B.H. Watts eds., *The Municipal Records of Bath 1189-1604* (n.d.), Appendix A, 67. For an example of the Corporation's aggressive exploitation of its properties in Broad Street see PRO, C3/301/19.

THE AVON NAVIGATION
AND THE INLAND PORT OF BATH

Brenda J. Buchanan

> Boats of burden used of old to carry goods from Bristol to
> Bath, until the river was obstructed by wears, mills, &c.[1]

This observation by the late eighteenth-century historian of Bristol, William
Barrett, shows the long-standing importance of the River Avon as a means of
transport, and suggests that the problems of navigation arose not from any
natural difficulties such as the river silting up or meandering in its course,
but from the man-made obstacles presented by the construction of weirs to
provide power and to facilitate fishing. These alternative uses must have
been well-established by the middle decades of the fourteenth century for
the removal of such barriers was first ordered in 1372.[2] In theory public rivers
were common highways, maintained in the country by the owners or
occupiers of adjacent lands, and in urban areas by the churchwardens of the
parishes through which they ran such as that of St Michael in Bath.[3] In practice,
the importance of this source of power and food was so great that water was
impounded for this purpose by barriers which then formed a great hindrance
to trade such as that between Bristol and Bath, described in 1411 as involving
the carriage of wine, corn, salt, wool, skins of wool, cloth and osiers.[4]

These problems came to be of more than purely local interest in the
seventeenth century when the strengthening of the national well-being was
sought through improvements which would help to make England strong
in relation to her neighbours and competitors, especially the Dutch. This
point was made by John Taylor, the waterman and innkeeper, poet and
pamphleteer, who urged the removal of obstructions from English rivers in
imitation of the 'industrious Netherlanders'. He claimed that:

> Thus men would be employ'd, and horse preserv'd
> And all the country at cheape rates be serv'd.

and asked the rhetorical question,

> Shall private persons for their gainfull use
> Ingrosse the water and the land abuse?[5]

Taylor was no taproom theorist for in 1641 he travelled by scull between the Thames and the Severn, and published that year a description of his undertaking. The experience of sculling along the Avon between Bath and Bristol led him to recommend in the *Last Voyage* that locks should be made 'at west Hanham weare, and at Kenisham (with 4 or 5 places more) for the river doth offer God's blessing to the peoples mouthes, if they would but open their lippes to receive them'.[6]

John Taylor's endeavours also gave rise to the suggestion that it might be possible to provide a link between rivers by means of a navigable cut, a far-sighted idea which was developed in the 1650s by Francis Mathew, who again emphasised that if England were to become a great nation she must imitate the then commercially supreme Dutch. He wrote that,

> The River Avon of Bristol may be ... made navigable from Bristol to Calne, or to Mamsbury in Wiltshire, and by cutting a graft of five miles, or thereabout ... may take its journey ... from Mamesbury to Leshlade in Oxfordshire, and there salute the river Isis already navigable, which so delivers itself into the Thames, and bring the trade of Ireland, the rich fruits of Cornwall, Devon and Somerset, Mendip Hills, and Wales ... as well as the intervening countryes, to the Cityes of Bristol and London ... and back again at will.[7]

But despite the example of the industrious Dutch, who were much admired for their hydraulic skills; the French, who built canals throughout the seventeenth century; and the Germans, whose Frederick William Canal, named after the Great Elector, was opened in 1669, the practical English concentrated on the more mundane task of making rivers navigable. This was achieved first in the south with schemes such as that for the Wey Navigation from the Thames to Guildford (1651-3), and then later in the north, where the newly awakening economic activity led to undertakings such as the improvement of the River Don that began in 1726. The work on the Bristol Avon in the 1720s was therefore against this trend,[8] although the delay was in no way due to a lack of interest in the idea.

Throughout the seventeenth century, schemes to improve the navigation of the River Avon were promoted and failed. By Letters Patent from James I in 1619 for example, the Mayor and Corporation of Bath secured the right to make the Avon navigable between their city and Bristol, but nothing came of this, nor of other schemes floated in the 1650s and 1660s.[9] Perhaps feeling that at the end of the century some special achievement must be recorded, the Corporation of Bath made a sustained effort in the 1690s to secure an Act of Parliament authorizing the improvement of the Avon. Leave to initiate proceedings in Parliament was granted on 30 December 1695, and on 29 January 1696 the Corporation agreed that one of its members, Mr Robert Chapman, should travel to London to solicit the Bill.[10] The course of this proposal may be traced in the Journal of the House of Commons. After the second reading there was a very close division of the House, with 81 votes for the yeas and 74 for the noes. The Bill was then committed to thirty-eight Members of Parliament (including Lord Pawlet as a rare Somerset peer), to which number could be added all those serving for the counties of Somerset, Wiltshire and Gloucestershire. Petitions from the region began to flow in, twenty in all. These are doubly interesting, both as evidence of the enthusiasm with which the parliamentary procedures, only fully established with the accession of William and Mary in 1689, were now being embraced, and as an indication of the conflicting interests locked in battle. Opponents of the Bill ranged from the gentry and farmers who feared for the value of their land and of their goods at market, to the owners of six of the mills on the river (producing dye-woods, grist and paper, and fulling cloth), who feared for their livelihood, as did the bakers of Bristol. The trading interests were in favour, as was shown in petitions from (in the order received), Warminster, Corsham, Chippenham, Calne, Devizes, Bradford, Trowbridge, Frome, Phillips-Norton, Bristol and the parts of Gloucestershire near Bath. But the old vested interests won and the proposals fizzled out.[11]

However the Corporation of Bath succeeded in promoting another Bill, which reached the statute books in 1712 (10 Anne c.2). Their success in securing this legislation may be interpreted as part of the shift in influence beginning to take place as the towns and ports, so dependent on the development of transport systems, asserted themselves against those whose interests lay in maintaining the *status quo,* like the old landed order and the millowners. The Act shows the extent to which the fortunes of Bath, especially as a growing fashionable resort, were felt to be tied up with the facilities provided by both the river and the roads, for the preamble states that the opening of a river passage between Bath and Hanham Mills near Bristol will be

> very beneficial to Trade, commodious and convenient for the Persons of Quality and Strangers (whose Resort thither is the principal Support of the said City of Bath), advantageous to the Poor, and convenient for the carriage of Free-stone, Wood, Timber, and other Goods and Merchandizes, to and from the said Cities and ports

adjacent, and will very much tend to the employing and increase of Watermen and Seamen, and be a means to preserve the Highways near and leading to the said City of Bath (which formerly being made ruinous and almost impassable are now repairing at a very great Charge).

But the 'new order' remained somewhat diffident about expressing its influence, perhaps because Bath Council's corporate status made it difficult for it to act decisively in matters such as the essential negotiations with riverside landowners. That problem and the continuing opposition of millers, farmers, maltsters and road carriers, as well as of those dependent on the resort who felt that the promised 'great Concourse of People' might be detrimental to the well-being of the aristocratic visitors, meant that the Council found itself unable to capitalize on the legislation it had secured. It was therefore not until these powers were handed over to a group of independent and entrepreneurially-minded proprietors in the mid-1720s that the improvement of the River Avon began.

On 17 June 1724 the Corporation agreed to grant the powers conferred by the act of 1712 for making the Avon navigable from Bath to Hanham's Mill to a new body of proprietors.[12] They met in Bath on 31 December 1724 and appointed as their treasurers Dr Charles Bave (a Bath physician), Thomas Attwood (plumber and glazier of Bath) and Ralph Allen (of whom more later). Their assistants were to be Thomas Tyndall (a Bristol merchant and shipowner who had established logwood mills at Swineford), Milo Smith (a stone quarrier, later bought out by Ralph Allen), Francis Bave (brother of Charles and a Bath apothecary), and John Hobbs (a Bristol timber merchant).[13] The last-named is often credited with the leading role in this enterprise,[14] but that judgement may give him more credit than he deserves. John Hobbs certainly had an eye to the house-building market in Bath, and he also seized the opportunity in 1725 to contract to provide timber for the locks, but by November of that year he was already falling behind with his dues, and he had died by the early 1730s. He was replaced by Joseph Jones, another Bristol timber merchant, so the Bristol connection remained a small but important part of the proprietorship. As well as Hobbs and Jones, it included two copper manufacturers, Robert Coster of the Bristol family firm and Dr John Lane, a lawyer concerned with works in Swansea; John Hickes, an African trader; James Hardwick, who later negotiated with the riverside owners and may have been an attorney; and Thomas Tyndall, already noted. The leading representatives of the

Bath interest included its Members of Parliament, Field Marshal Wade and John Codrington, and leaders of its local aristocracy, the Duke of Beaufort and his brother Lord Noel Somerset. They, together with three other gentlemen, signed the deeds of conveyance from Bath Council in March 1725.[15] Despite the importance of these men, and of those making up the Bristol group, the proprietors came to be dominated by Ralph Allen, who was not only an initiator of the venture but was also of continuing significance as its chief treasurer. He was a successful Bath entrepreneur with a lucrative control of the mail by-passing London. To this source of profit must be added his stone quarries whose market stood to be extended beyond Bath by the improved navigability of the Avon, in which he had therefore a considerable personal interest.

The thirty-two shares were initially limited to one per proprietor, with capital to be called up as work on the Avon progressed. This would have limited Allen's influence, but he overcame the restriction in an ingenious manner. From the surviving documents it is possible to show that he also enrolled as proprietors his wife Elizabeth, mother Gertrude, nephew Philip, sister-in-law Sarah Hudson, and brothers-in-law Anthony Roderick Buckeridge and Charles Holder. When the last-named withdrew, that share was taken over by Ralph's brother Philip, and on his mother's death her share went to his father.[16]

As has been noted, Ralph Allen was appointed one of several treasurers at the first meeting of the co-partners on 31 December 1724. But his seniority was demonstrated at the next meeting on 1 January 1725, when it was decided that a newly-purchased iron chest should be 'lodged in ye poste offis or in ye dwelling hous of Mr Ralph Allin as he Shall find moste Convenient'. The iron chest deserves mention for it shows how finances were handled in this region for much of the eighteenth century. When the proprietors answered a call for funds in September 1725 for example, £420 was 'put in the Chest' as part of the sum of at least £12,000 which passed through Allen's hands in the first ten years of the venture. The image of his private and public affairs being funded from many such coffers is not fanciful. His biographer Benjamin Boyce writes that the architect John Wood's fears about the financing of the great mansion of Prior Park in the mid-1730s were lulled when 'Allen led him into the room where he kept his money and opened chest after chest full of guineas'. Boyce feels this story to be 'not a little improbable', but the evidence from the minutes of the Avon Navigation suggests the likely accuracy of Wood's observation, although the chests may have contained more than Allen's personal reserves.[17]

In addition to the capital sum invested by the proprietors, Ralph Allen also had responsibility for handling the revenue from the tolls, authorized by the Act of 1712 and levied on goods and passengers carried by vessels using the improved River Avon. In the 1730s these averaged over £700 per year.[18] The reward for handling such current funds was the opportunity to put them also to private use, and although there is no suggestion of malpractice on Ralph Allen's part, others had lower standards, as was discovered in 1786 after the deaths of the then joint treasurers, Leonard Coward, linen draper, and Richard Attwood, plumber.[19] This experience notwithstanding, the tolls levied on users of the Navigation provided a steady source of income, above £1,000 per year in the later 1760s and 1780s, and early 1790s. But although efficiently run the concern remained a local one, with the proprietors deaf to the pleas for an extension towards London which surfaced intermittently, especially from the Bristol merchants anxious to extend their area of trade. They had no success until the early 1790s when, due to the easier investment conditions of those years and the contagion of the 'canal mania', the Kennet & Avon, Somersetshire Coal, and Dorset & Somerset Canals were all promoted in moves which are however beyond our present scope.

Meanwhile, having called up the first round of subscriptions, the proprietors quickly embarked upon their task of making the river navigable. The weir at Pulteney Bridge was to mark the limit of their efforts, and although this structure has since been rebuilt it still provides a reminder of the barriers of earlier times. Two mills formerly operated here, one on the abbey and one on the Bathwick side, both drawing water from above the dam by means of leats or culverts in a pattern which was repeated at intervals along the course of the river. The traditional response to such weirs had been to haul boats around the obstruction, or to wait until millers were willing to release a 'flash' or flush of water by removing paddles set between stakes of wood (such as may possibly be seen in fig. 1), to equalize levels. Both methods were unsatisfactory and the engineering solution adopted on this and other Navigations was to by-pass the weirs by the construction of lateral cuts, where vessels could be held securely in pound locks whilst water levels were adjusted. The extent of the problem facing the proprietors may be seen in fig. 2, which shows the length of the river concerned. The Avon is tidal to Hanham, but from that point to Bath, cuts and locks had to be made to negotiate the following changes in waterlevel: Hanham (a few inches); Keynsham (6ft 10ins); Swineford (3ft 1in); Saltford (3ft 10ins); Kelston (3ft 1in); and Weston (9ft 3ins).

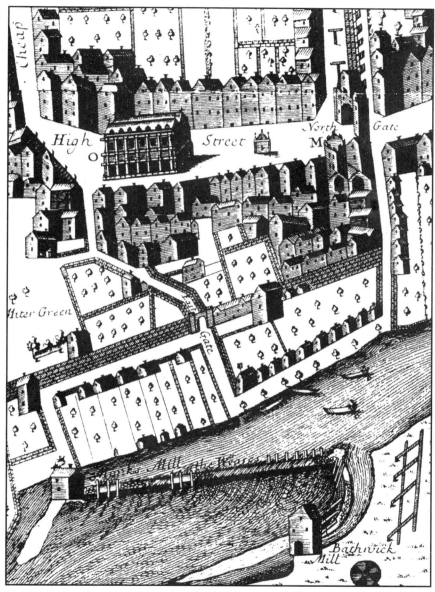

1. Detail from Joseph Gilmore's *Plan*, 1694, showing the weir (possibly with a flash lock) which was to mark the upper limit of the Avon Navigation.

2. The River Avon made navigable to Bath, 1724-27. (From Archibald Robertson, A Topographical Survey of the Great Road from London to Bath and Bristol (1792), plate 11)

At their meetings in March and April 1725 the proprietors agreed to employ John Hoare of Newbury in the 'Direction and Chief management of the Works', and they wrote asking him to bring 'Proper Instrumts ... for taking of a Thorough Survey of the River. To mark out all the Grounds wch will be anyway made use of in this undertaking and to prepare an Estimate of the whole Expence'. He was offered 9 guineas per week for his attendance and journeyings, for which two days per week were allowed. In recognition of the fact that after his successful work on the Kennet Navigation (1718-23) John Hoare's expertise was much in demand, it was agreed that his assistant Mr Downs should be in charge in his absence, thus establishing Hoare as an early consulting engineer.[20] Work was to start first at Hanham Mill, for which timber was to be purchased by John Hobbs, together with a boat or barge of 15 to 20 tons for the 'Service of the Works'. Edward Marchant was to be chief mason there, and to do any other 'Casual Business which may be required of him at the Lime Kilns, Quarrys, Locks &c For two Guineas a Week during his attendance'. In May 1725 the proprietors supported an experiment to determine the best way of raising heavy materials, by crane or by haulage. They ordered 'that one Tackle or Winless be put up and made use of at the Cut by Hanham's Mills and that the Sloptes now made Use of in that Place for the Dispatch of that Work be Likewise Continued that it may by Experience appear which of these Methods is most Expeditious and Serviceable to the Undertaking'. The proprietors were clearly anxious to start securing some revenue from the tolls as soon as possible, for on 5 October 1725 they resolved that 'the lock at Hanham Mills be open'd with all Expedition and that fourpence p Tun be demanded for all goods passing through the said Lock'. They were authorized to charge 5s per ton and 6d per person on the whole Navigation, so 4d per ton would be a fair charge for a very limited service.

Hanham was within Bristol's rather than Bath's sphere of influence. Its mills mentioned above supplied that market with flour; from 1698 the Bristol Water Company piped and pumped water from this site to Crews Hole and thence to a reservoir at Lawrence Hill, helping to provide for the city for a century; and several wealthy Bristol merchants settled here, including from the 1630s the Creswick(e)s at Hanham Court.[21] This litigious family and other landowners created difficulties for the proprietors, which show that in addition to the engineering challenges they also had to face problems arising from the need to acquire land for locks, wharves, bridges and watercourses. To help resolve these problems however they were able to look for advice to certain special

commissioners, named in the original Act of Parliament. These were all
men of substance in the region, whose number could be supplemented
by further nominees of similar standing in place of those who had died,
and whose function was to adjudicate on the value of property taken or
damaged. It is a measure of the importance attributed to this function
that forty-five eminent gentleman attended the first meeting on 23 April
1725. The list from which they were drawn included the Duke of Beaufort,
the mayors of Bristol and Bath, and well-established country gentlemen
such as Henry Creswick Esq. of Hanham. By 22 November 1725 he
had made known his objections to what amounted to the compulsory
purchase of three-quarters of an acre of his land in Sydenham Mead, for
the purpose of building a wharf at Keynsham. The undertakers of the
Navigation decided that a legal instrument for conveying this property
must be speedily engrossed, so that the land could be included in the
commissioners' inquisition into all the difficult cases, which was due to
be held. The dispute was resolved by this means, but had there been no
system of arbitration, established by Act of Parliament and administered
by social equals, to which both landowners and undertakers could appeal,
then the work on the Avon Navigation would have proceeded much more
slowly.

The cut which was eventually made through disputed land at Sydenham
Mead is shown in fig. 3. This section of an estate map also shows the
great brass mills at Keynsham, established in 1708, together with the weir
which allowed water to be diverted to service the eight undershot wheels
that supplied power to the works.[22] This was the second lock to be tackled
by the proprietors, and here the engineering problems were exacerbated
by flooding. On 5 October 1725 the Committee were presented with a
letter sent on 18 September on their behalf by Thomas Attwood, Ralph
Allen and Francis Bave to Mr Hoare of Newbury, explaining that:

> The Water breaks in so fast upon the Low part of our Work at
> Keynsham that there is an absolute Necessity for the screw or some
> other Engine to be Erected at that Place. Mr Downs's letter will
> acquaint you with the Draught of the Three Common Pumps that are
> now upon that Place wth his Sentements of the additionall helps that
> is Necessary for the Draining of the Work, but that no disapointment
> may retard an affair of this Consequence we have sent Mr Marchant
> on Purpose with this letter who will acquaint you fully with the
> manner of the obstruction, advise with and be directed by you for the
> Imediat removall of it, and as the works in that Cut are now in

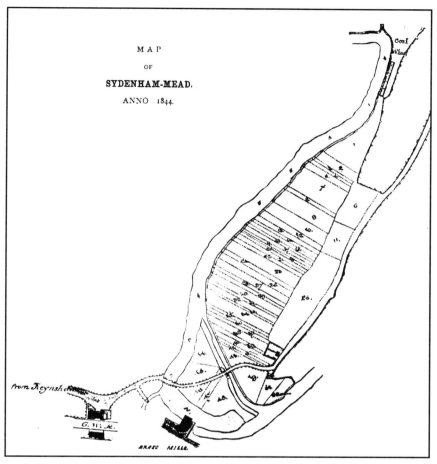

3. Estate map of Sydenham Mead, 1844, showing the weir serving the brass mills and the cut through private property owned in part by the Creswick family. *(From H.T. Ellacombe, History of the Parish of Bitton (Exeter, 1883), plate vi)*

considerable forwardness we must desire that you will soon be with us to direct ye finishing of that and Hanhams Lock, but if your affairs upon the Newbury River will not admit of your speedy attendance here, we must desire you to give Mr Marchant full directions for his Proceeding til we can have your Personal Assistance that our Undertaking may not Suffer by any Unnecessary delays.

[*A postcript notes*:] We hear that there are now some Screw Engines upon the Newbury River and not in use, if there shou'd be any that would be of Service to us we must desire your assistance for a reasonable Purchass, this appears to us the Speediest Method.

On 1 November the Committee ordered that Mr Hoare should give instructions 'to Mr Padmore for a Draught of the Gates to be erected at Keynsham', and asked for a review of the siting of the wharf at Keynsham, which they thought inconvenient. This may well have been because of the then still unresolved difficulties caused by Henry Creswick. Perhaps it was these planning uncertainties, plus the flooding at the Keynsham Lock, together with the onset of winter, that caused the Committee to order on 9 November 1725 that 'the Whole Work be Suspended till a proper Season offers the next Spring and that Mr Hoare or Mr Downs do forthwith make a Draft of the River from Swinford to Bath and make out proper Places at Swinford and Bath for the Wharfs to be made there'.

Upstream of Keynsham the mills at Bitton, mid-way between Bristol and Bath, presented lesser problems because they were sited on the River Boyd rather than the Avon. Although only a small tributary of the main river it provided power for several undertakings, most notably the Bitton Mill brass works. This arrangement meant there was no weir across the Avon requiring the construction of a lock; however a wharf built for the shipment of goods drew the mills of the Golden Valley into the network using the Navigation. Bitton is also of more general interest because from 1758 to 1765 the architect John Wood the younger rented a house here, situated between the church and the Avon, and called The Rectory. There are intriguing hints that changes he made here anticipated some of his later work at, for example, the Upper Assembly Rooms in Bath. Despite the attractions of the village, and its location on the turnpike road between Bath and Bristol, it is difficult to see why Wood chose to live there. There was a slight professional link as his father, John Wood the elder, had been associated with the construction of the Avon Navigation, though probably without the responsibilities that have sometimes been claimed for him. Payments 'for diging' in the middle months of 1727 for example show a concern with manual work, at a time when the Bristol engineer John Padmore was through his technical skills playing an important part in the execution of the 'grand design'.[23] Wood the younger may however have been drawn by a longer-standing connection, arising from the origins of the family. These have always been a mystery, and it used to be suggested that Wood the elder came from Yorkshire or Cheshire. It now seems that his father

George and a brother worked for him in Bath, suggesting a more local if still unspecified background. Firm evidence is lacking, but it may be significant that the Bitton parish registers from the 1620s to nearly 1720 show entries relating to a Wood family, including as a matter of particular interest a George Wood, whose daughter was baptized in 1674.[24] Perhaps like other skilled craftsmen they moved from the countryside in the early eighteenth century, into an urban market hungry for their talents.

After the suspension of activities other than surveying in November 1725, work was resumed in the following spring and a lock and wharf were soon underway at Swineford. Here the mills causing the obstruction were owned by Coster's Copper Company, and progress was eased by the fact that a family member of this partnership, Robert Coster, was also a proprietor of the Navigation. Costers had taken over a 'double tucking mill' in 1709, adapting it to function as a rolling mill for the company which later became the Joseph Percival & Copper Company, and then the John Freeman & Copper Company. In 1840 new premises were added under the last-named owners and most of the surviving buildings date from then, having become in turn a lead works, a flock mill and most recently a light engineering plant.

It is entirely typical of the manufacturing units along the whole line of the river that buildings should be modified and their function changed over the years. In the approaches to Saltford, for example, a leather mill on the south or Somerset side of the river had been transformed into a paper mill before the premises were acquired in the late 1780s by the Bristol Brass Company, possibly in order to secure the water rights across the whole river. This was desirable because their mill, on the northern or Gloucestershire side, which had been a fulling mill before becoming a copper and brass battery mill, had substantial power requirements. Battery work stopped here in the 1840s but two annealing towers still survive. To by-pass the fine curving weir the Saltford lock was built on the Somerset bank of the river. The papermaker's house survives as *The Jolly Sailor Inn*. Further upstream, at the other end of the village, the now-restored brass battery mill remained in operation in the first quarter of the twentieth century, sheet brass being rolled here in the 1920s. The by-passing of its weir led to the building of Kelston Lock on the Gloucestershire side, after which the route goes upstream to Bath, past the villages of Weston and Twerton.

On the western outskirts of Bath, river traffic was impeded by two weirs which served mills engaged in the textile and metals industries, at Weston on the north bank and Twerton on the south. The proprietors of the Navigation decided on a bold straight cut on the Weston side, which isolated a pocket of land in the course of by-passing the weirs. A small bridge still gives access to what became known as Dutch Island by its association with the continental workers employed in the manufacture of copper and brass at the nearby Weston Mill. By 1813 edge-tools were being produced there, and by 1840 a logwood mill had been established. Later however this became the site of one of the major cloth mills which contributed so much to Bath's prosperity in the nineteenth and first part of the twentieth century, the others being at Twerton.[25]

The completion of the Navigation at the end of 1727 was marked by the building of a quay downstream of the old Bath Bridge, on the town side of the river, though this location was only chosen after serious consideration had been given to other locations upstream of the bridge. For some years from 1629 a site was reserved for the construction of a harbour when the Avon was made passable, on the town side of the river by the ditch (marked by a line of trees on the front cover illustration) above Bath Bridge. In the 1720s a quay by the present Recreation Ground was considered but there were obvious disadvantages in requiring vessels to sail under the bridge, although Ralph Allen operated his own wharf at nearby Dolemeads, to which, from 1731, stone was brought by the tramway from his mines at Combe Down. That for the early building of Bath had then only to be taken across the river to Monks Mill and rolled up a sloping road made for the purpose. The Avon Navigation quay was finally completed in 1729 below Bath Bridge. John Wood observed that the 'Key ... a large Terrass ... extending four hundred and eighty three Feet in Length, by ninety seven Feet in Breadth, in one Part, contains eleven Houses', presumably warehouses.[26]

The system of locks, cuts and wharves was now complete, and the only other major works of construction concerned the New Bridge and the towpath, both of which came after the initial work had been undertaken.

The New Bridge did not form part of the initial plan for the Avon Navigation because the Act of 1712 had allowed the proprietors a choice. They were either to:

> preserve and maintain the Ford called Newton's Ford (as it now is) fit and convenient for Horses, Waggons, and other Carriages to pass over, or else build and erect, at their own proper Costs and Expences, a bridge over the said River Avon at or near the said Newton's Ford, fit and convenient for Horses, Waggons, or other Carriages to pass over, and keep the same in repair.

It is not surprising that they chose the first option for fords were still widely used in the eighteenth century, until the increase of the weight of goods in waggons and the number of passengers in coaches began to make them impracticable. But when the river was deepened as an aid to navigation and it became clear that Newton's Ford would have to be bridged, the task fell to the Navigators by the terms of the Act despite the growing tendency for the county authorities to meet this responsibility.[27] The upkeep of country bridges in Somerset was sometimes placed in the hands of the turnpike trustees of the road concerned, with costs met by the county, but although the Bath Trust was already established it had as yet no role in this matter for the link between the Upper and Lower Bristol Roads was still to be turnpiked.[28]

The work of construction was undertaken in the mid-1730s, and on 18 January 1736 a payment of £851 4s 6d to Ralph Allen 'for the Newton Bridge' was recorded in the current Cash Book. This was 'as pr contract' and included stone steps to the bridge, and a wall along it.[29] Ralph Allen's Clerk of Works, Richard Jones, later stated in his manuscript autobiography that he had 'built the New Bridge over Newton,which was done in two years to my desire',[30] a claim which may come to seem more like an admission in view of the fate which befell the structure in 1774. Incessant rain in early March led to a great flood, such that after four days, as was reported in the *Bath Chronicle* of 17 March 1774, the water was nearly 12 perpendicular feet above the bed of the river, the Avon Street area was submerged, the lower road to Bristol was like a 'rapid river', and the centre arch of the New Bridge at Newton had given way, preventing any passage over it. This disaster affected the Bath Trustees closely because the turnpike link between the Upper and Lower Bristol Roads, in which the Newton Bridge played an esssential part, had been established in 1759. They therefore commissioned an investigation by Mr Esau Reynolds of Trowbridge.

Mr Reynold's report, presented in July 1774, reassured the Trustees that the road they had built on either side of the bridge was not a detriment to it but a support. The bridge had fallen because of inherent weaknesses. It 'was not built of a sufficient Breadth, neither was the Height enough from the under side of the Center Arch to the Roadway over it'. The Trustees informed the Proprietors of the Navigation of this report and asked for their proposed plans and costings. They learnt that the Navigators were considering a rebuilding and widening which would extend the bridge to 24 feet across 'from Outside to Outside' and said that if this were undertaken they would build and repair the land anchors, and pay one-third of the rebuilding costs. The offer was rejected.[31] It has hitherto seemed likely that the Navigators

4. The first Newton Bridge from a watercolour by Anthony Devis, entitled 'In the road from Bath to Bristol'. *(Reproduced by courtesy of the Harris Museum and Art Gallery, Preston Borough Council)*

preferred instead to repair the original bridge to lesser specifications, especially as in the early 1830s it had to be substantially worked upon and widened.[32] However, the paintings of Anthony Devis, exhibited at the Victoria Art Gallery in Bath in December 1993, may throw new light on this problem. Devis was a travelling landscape artist who satisfied the tastes of his patrons with delicate but realistic paintings of their houses and estates, and kept alive his own interests with informal works executed 'in the road'. One of these, undated, shows a bridge 'in the road from Bath to Bristol', for which the first Newton Bridge with its flight of steps (to the right in fig. 4), parapet and high central arch, essential for the passage of boats but prejudicial to its stability, seems the most fitting candidate.[33] Indeed, once this link has been suggested it would seem to follow that John Wood's description of the bridge in the mid-eighteenth century as spanning the river with three arches, of which the height of the middle one above the approach roads rendered the whole not only dangerous but also 'the shadow of a good Design ignorantly applied',[34]

5. The North Parade, Bath, showing men hauling a barge on the River Avon. Dated 1773, this tinted etching is one of a set of eight by John Robert Cozens. *(Reproduced by courtesy of the Victoria Art Gallery, Bath & North East Somerset Council)*

refers to the first bridge rather than its elegant and surviving replacement. If so, it may be that in the Devis painting we have found the previously unidentified first Newton bridge.

The second work of late construction concerns the creation of a towpath in the early nineteenth century. Before that, movement downstream was generally aided by the current, and upstream by the use of sails to harness the prevailing westerly winds. When that failed, men were roped up to haul the boats. The Act had given the Navigators powers to set out 'Towing Paths and Ways for Men, for haling or drawing of Boats, Barges, Lighters', but the clause included no reference to horses. By chance an illustration of this procedure is included on one of the many paintings of Bath in the eighteenth century (fig. 5), but the only account of it found so far comes from the diary of an American visitor to London in the mid-1730s, who travelled up the river to Twickenham for a fine lunch which included 'Salmon Caut in the river Thams', green peas and a bottle or two of wine. He noted that in the higher reaches the large flat-bottomed barges of about 120 feet or longer had:

a mast Obout 30 feet long Situated Pretty nigh the middle of the Vessell, at the top of which there is a ring through which they reave the rope and fasten it to Something at the stern. The other End goes to the Shore; it is about 100 faddom long. By this rope men with Sort of Collers made on purpose, which goes under one Arm and over t'other and fastened to the rope, pull the boat along. To Some of these Barges they have 16 or 18 men, to others not more than 6, and, when the[y] Come to a Certain hight where the stream runes too strong for the men, they Hire horses to Draw in the place of men.[35]

But on the Avon that alternative was not available until the passing of the amendment Act of 1807 (47 Geo III c.129). The advantages seem obvious, and were set out by the proprietors of the Kennet & Avon Canal Company (not those of the Navigation who remained opposed to the innovation), in a petition of February of that year. They argued that:

if power was given to make a Horse-towing Path from Bath to Hanham's Mills, to haul Boats, Lighters, and other Vessels, with horses and other beasts, the said river would be navigated with greater expedition, certainty and convenience, and at less expense.[36]

It would also of course confer an advantage on their own special concern, the Kennet & Avon Canal, built over the years 1794-1810 in order to create a great west-east link between the navigable rivers Avon and Kennet, and so between Bristol and London.

The Commons Journal shows that the petition was referred to a small committee of the House which included Mr Charles Dundas, MP, JP, and Chairman of the Kennet & Avon Canal Company. But despite this favourable circumstance all did not go smoothly, for on 24 April 1807 an opposing petition was received which showed that the local landowners and major manufacturers based on the river had doubts about the Bill. The former feared that the heavy horses would have an adverse effect on their land, and asked that their fences should continue to the water's edge although this would require them to be jumped – a proposal not as improbable as it might seem in view of Constable's portrayal of the *Leaping Horses* of the River Stour. The manufacturers united in opposition included 'Messrs Harfords & Bristol Brass Company, Messrs John Freeman & Copper Company of the said City of Bristol, Messrs Pollard, Jackson & Schimmelpenning of the said City of Bristol, Drysalters, Messrs Francis Naish, Clothier, and Ebenezer Browne the yr, Clothier, both of the parish of Twerton, Somerset, and Richard Sheldon Collicott, of the parish of Weston, said county, Clothier'. Despite these representations the Act received the Royal Assent on 14 August 1807, but only after the Commons had accepted two amendments introduced by the Lords. The first stated that the horse towing path was not to be made or used until the Kennet & Avon Canal had been completed and made navigable between Newbury and Bath; and the second said that the proprietors were not to make use of any part of any building on the line of the new towing path without first purchasing the whole, if the owners wished. And so, on the Avon Navigation, the 'strain, force and pain' of man haulage at last gave way to horse power.[37]

The goods hauled on the river in one-masted barges of 40 to 140 tons at such severe personal cost included copper and brass from Cornwall and South Wales for the manufacturing firms mentioned, with the finished products carried back to Bristol; building materials such as iron and slate from Wales, pennant sandstone paving slabs from Bristol, and deal from the Baltic and Scandinavian countries; ironware for cooking utensils and kitchen ranges from Coalbrookdale; coal from South Wales; grain and other food from the Midlands; and luxuries such as wine, chiefly from the Iberian Peninsula. That the commodities carried were for domestic as well as commercial consumption is shown by Dr Charles Bave's cargo of port wine from Lisbon in 1731, bought through the Bristol merchant John Lason.[38] But the Avon Navigation acted as more than a conduit by which bulky goods could be brought upriver more cheaply from coastal and international sources, it also allowed the inland city of Bath to act as a true port by extending the markets to which its goods could be despatched by water. This meant for example that for eight decades before the Kennet & Avon Canal was built, the splendid freestone used in many of the public buildings and great houses of the eighteenth century could be carried away by river. Charges were imposed on goods according to the tolls set out in the Act. They were not to exceed 5s per ton from Hanham Mills to Bath, and to be modified proportionately for 'any greater or lesser Weight or Distance of Place'.

The comparable rate for passengers was 6d, a provision which serves to remind us that the Navigation was conceived as a way of providing transport for passengers as well as goods. The superior speed offered by stage coaches from the later decades of the eighteenth century and railways from the 1830s, came to detract from the service offered by rivers and canals, but in the early years of the Avon Navigation an important form of transport was provided for the public. The person credited with

BRENDA J. BUCHANAN

6. 'A View of the *Jolly Sailor* at Saltford Weir and Lock' on the Avon Navigation; English Provincial School, c.1728, oil on panel. *(Reproduced by courtesy of A.Csaky)*

making the first journey between Bristol and Bath was Lord Falmouth, on 3 January 1728, the works having been completed late in 1727. The Navigation received not only the noble but also the royal seal of approval a few months later when on 9 May 1728 the Princess Amelia, daughter of George II, whose dislike of road transport was well known, made the journey to Bristol in what was described as a 'roomy wherry', decorated for the occasion. Indeed, the smooth journey offered by the waterway seems to have been so attractive that even before the whole Navigation was finished, river boats were plying their trade on completed sections. *Farley's Newspaper* of 2 September 1727 for example, records an accident to 'the new Passage Boat between Bristol and Twerton'.[39]

We are fortunate that something of the bustle and excitement of the early days survives in a painting of naïve charm which hung for more than 260 years at *The Jolly Sailor* inn, formerly the miller's house, at Saltford weir. As fig. 6 shows, the artist has attempted to depict not only the miller's house with its sloping lawn, but also the lock with its steps up from the river and the keeper working the downstream gate. The level of activity on the river suggests that the painting dates from at least 1728, when it was fully navigable. On the right, men are shown hauling a vessel into place for the lock, whilst the barge to the left of the picture has the advantage of the wind and the flow of the river, removing the need for manual effort. The flags with their different emblems perhaps identified the various firms which operated regularly. The two boats within the lock are representative of the traffic on the river. A cargo-carrying barge is dragging a smaller one, perhaps bearing blocks of stone, and a passenger boat with its cabin lies aft.[40] That passengers travelled in comfort is confirmed by an announcement in the *Gloucestershire Journal* of 15 April 1740, that Samuel Tonkins had added three new boats to his stock, 'with a house on each, with sash windows'. Two boats plied daily, the journey took about four hours, and the fare was one shilling. The Tonkins family remained in business for some time, the *Bath & Bristol Guide* of 1755 for example recording that 'Wherries for Pleasuring, and for Bristol, may be had of Mr Tonkins, at the Vernon-Inn, near the Bridge, Bath'.

Despite the success of these early years the proprietors of the Avon Navigation failed to take any interest in the schemes floated between its opening and the construction of the Kennet & Avon Canal at the end of the eighteenth century, to make the river accessible to its higher reaches, to Melksham or Chippenham. This unwillingness to extend their business may be understandable in terms of the welcome financial returns already secured by their waterway monopoly between Bath and Bristol, but in the long run it meant that the Avon Navigation ceased to have a future as an independent body. Control was gradually assumed by the Kennet & Avon Canal Company by the simple expedient of buying up shares as they became available. By 1796 they held a majority, though to their frustration one shareholder held out until the 1860s.

As with all social and economic changes which can be portrayed as operating to the public good as well as providing a private profit, the 'improvements' here described brought disadvantages as well as advantages. The regulation of the river by the introduction of tolls on what had rightly been seen as a public right of way, of the same standing as the King's Highways before the turnpike trusts began to exercise their control over them, enraged some of the poorer members of local society. Not only were the tolls an affront, but the river improvements also allowed little local monopolies to be broken, to the disadvantage of such as the Kingswood colliers who objected strongly to the coal which could now be brought cheaply into the Bath area from across the Severn estuary. And just as there were outbreaks of destructive violence against the apparatus of the turnpike trusts, especially the gates and tollhouses, so also the gates and locks on the river were threatened and attacked. Once again, some of the gentry were known to support these complaints, and it may place Henry Creswick of Hanham's quarrels with the Avon Navigators in a broader perspective if it is noted that a few years later, in 1734, he was obliged to write a letter asserting his innocence of this serious charge. Matters culminated in 1738 with the wrecking of the lock at Saltford, but although the rioters claimed that 300 men had wrought the damage, and that 1,000 were ready to act to stop the transport of coal by water, the movement died down.[41] Perhaps because these structures were less easy to tackle than those on the roads the destruction was neither so great nor so widespread, but this strong opposition serves as a reminder of the human perspective within which all changes to an established order should be viewed.

The completion of the Avon Navigation thus had a profound effect on the life and economy of Bath, challenging long-established markets and local monopolies and opening up the city to the stimulus of new patterns of national and international trade. As William Mathews (or Matthews), publisher of one of the longest and most complete series of directories in the country observed in the first *New Bristol Directory, 1793-4*, the river improvements had established Bath as 'a proper inland Port'.[42]

Notes

1   William Barrett, *The History and Antiquities of the City of Bristol* (Bristol,1789), pp.53-4.

2   Graham Boyes, 'The Legislative History of River Navigation and Canals, 1275-1603', *Journal of the Railway & Canal Historical Society*, Vol. 29, No. 136 (1987), pp.65-78.

3   W.T. Jackman, *The Development of Transportation in Modern England* (Cambridge, 1916), Vol.1, pp.22-8, 157-210; Rt. Rev. Bishop Hobhouse, *Churchwardens' Accounts of Croscombe, Pilton, Yatton, Tintinhull, Morebath & St Michael's, Bath, 1349-1560* (1890), pp.xv, 160, 170.

4   Boyes, 'Legislative History of River Navigation', p.77.

5   Quoted by T.S. Willan, *River Navigation in England, 1600-1750* (Oxford, 1936), p.6; see also his short account of 'Bath and the Navigation of the River Avon', *Proceedings of the Bath & District Branch of the Somerset Archaeology & Natural History Society* (1936), pp.139-40.

6   *John Taylor's Last Voyage* (1641), p.4.

7   Francis Mathew, *A Mediterranean Passage by Water from London to Bristol ...* (1655), quoted by Jackman, *Development of Transportation*, Vol. 1, pp.186-90.

8   Willan, *River Navigation*, pp.11-15.

9   John Latimer, *The Annals of Bristol* (Bristol, 1900-08), Vol. 1, The Seventeenth Century, pp.71, 268-9; Willan, *River Navigation*, pp.24-51, also 'Bath and the River Avon', pp.139-40.

10   Journal of the House of Commons, Vol. 11, 1693-97, 30 December 1695; Bath Record Office (BRO), Minute Book of Bath Council, Vol. 3, 1684-1711, 29 January 1695/6. Until the reform of the calendar in 1752 the New Year began on Lady Day, 25 March. In the footnotes both styles are shown, but in the text of the article the year is taken as running from 1 January.

11   Journal of the House of Commons, Vol. 11, 1693-97. 28 entries relate to this proposal, from 30 December 1695 to 26 January 1696/7.

12   BRO, Bath Council Minute Book, Vol. 4, 1711-28, 17 June 1724.

13   Public Record Office (PRO), Rail 805, Minute Book of Proprietors of the Avon Navigation, Vol. 1, 1724-27, 31 December 1724.

14   See, for example, Kenneth R. Clew, *The Kennet & Avon Canal* (Newton Abbot, 1968, second edition 1973), p.18.

15   PRO, Rail 805, Minute Book, Vol. 1. On 16 March 1724/5 it was decided to send the deeds to Oxford to be signed. By omitting to adjust the calendar Clew places this event and the engagement with John Hoare which followed, in 1724 rather than 1725, see *Kennet & Avon*, p.18.

16   PRO, Rail 805, Minute Book, Vol. 1, 31 December 1724, 2 February 1724/5, 1 December 1725. Further details of meetings and construction work are from the Minute Books unless stated otherwise.

17   Benjamin Boyce, *The Benevolent Man* (Cambridge, Mass., 1967), p.72, n.32.

18   See R.S. Neale, *Bath, 1680-1850* (1981), Appendix A, pp.384-90, for the revenue from the Avon Tolls in the eighteenth century.

19   Clew, *Kennet & Avon*, pp.21-2.

20   It is the view of the eminent civil engineer A.W. Skempton that John Ho(a)re
      was 'in the first rank among the navigation engineers'; see 'The Engineers
      of the English River Navigations, 1620-1760', *Transactions of the Newcomen
      Society*, Vol. 29 (1958), p.46.

21   Latimer, *Annals of Bristol*, Vol. 1, pp.468-9. For the Creswickes' lawsuits
      see W.J. Robinson, *West Country Manors* (Bristol, 1930), pp.82-3.

22   Joan Day, *Bristol Brass, a History of the Industry* (Newton Abbot, 1973)
      provides information on this and other brass and copper mills on the Avon.
      For an introduction to some of the surviving features and facilities on the
      former Avon Navigation, see Niall Allsop, *The Kennet & Avon Canal: a User's
      Guide to the Waterways between Reading and Bristol* (Bath, 1987).

23   PRO, Rail 805, Accountant's Records, Journal Vol. 20, 1725-63, fo.27. In
      his *Essay Towards a Description of Bath* (1749, second edition 1765,
      reprinted Bath, 1969), p.241, John Wood notes that he used labourers
      formerly employed on the Chelsea Waterworks for the digging of the
      Weston Cut, and that the time required was much reduced by their 'real
      Use of the Spade ... unknown in, or about the City'. In view of the
      advanced equipment used on this project this is an extraordinary claim,
      and raises the question of what was meant by the 'real Use of the
      Spade'. Wood's association with the Navigation was in any case short-
      lived, for when 'difficulties' arose in relation to that part of the Cut where
      the lock was to be built, the work of construction was assumed by
      Edward Marchant and his workmen. A Quaker of Bath, Marchant proved
      to be a reliable chief mason and contractor for the Navigation. Wood's
      short contract was terminated in July 1727. On the neglected engineer
      John Padmore, see R.A. Buchanan & Neil Cossons, *The Industrial
      Archaeology of the Bristol Region* (Newton Abbot, 1969). In addition to
      the Avon Navigation he worked on Ralph Allen's tramway and its
      cranes, the Great Crane for Bristol Docks, the construction of Sea Mills
      Dock near Bristol, and an 'atmospheric engine' to pump water from
      Hanham.

24   The most recent study, by Tim Mowl & Brian Earnshaw, *John Wood,
      Architect of Obsession* (Bath, 1988), makes no reference to a possible Bitton
      connection, but see C.P. Ketchley, 'John Wood the Younger of Bath and
      Bitton', *The Bath Critic*, Vol. 2, No. 7 (1952), pp.264-5.

25   See the article by Nicholas von Behr in this volume.

26   I am indebted to Mrs Marta Inskip for details of the 1629 and later
      transactions re this site. For an assessment of Ralph Allen's tramway,
      see Buchanan & Cossons, *The Bristol Region*, pp.202-3. For Wood's note on
      the quay, see his *Description of Bath*, p.331.

27   Jackman, *Development of Transportation*, pp.144-6.

28   For information on the Bath Trust, see B.J. Buchanan, 'The Evolution of
      the Turnpike Trusts: lessons from a case study', *Economic History Review*,
      2nd series, Vol. 39 (1986), pp.223-43 and 'The Great Bath Road, 1700-1830',
      Bath History, Vol. 4 (1992), pp.71-94.

29   PRO, Rail 805, Accountant's Records, Cash Book Vol. 23, 1725-44, fo.49.

30   W. Gregory, *Ralph Allen and Prior Park* (Bath, 1886), reproduces this

manuscript *verbatim*. See particularly p.39. I am grateful to Mr Philip Wooster for this reference.

31 Somerset Record Office, D/T/ba, 7, Minute Book, 1770-76. Entries for 2 July, 20 & 27 August, 10 & 17 September 1774. A committee to organize the making of a road each side of the New Bridge was appointed by the Turnpike Trustees on 2 March 1776.

32 Bryan Little, *Bath Portrait* (Bath, 1961), p.93; R. Angus Buchanan, 'The Bridges of Bath', *Bath History*, Vol. 3 (1990), pp.1-21.

33 The exhibition catalogue entitled *Anthony Devis (1729-1816)* was compiled by Stephen Whittle, Keeper of Fine Art at the Harris Museum and Art Gallery, Preston, Lancashire. I should like to thank Mr Whittle and his colleagues for their advice, especially that the painting may date from the mid-1770s to mid-1780s. It may therefore have been painted just before the bridge collapsed.

34 Wood, *Description of Bath*, p.372.

35 Robert Hunter Morris, 'An American in London, 1735-1736', diary edited by Beverley McAnear, *Pennsylvania Magazine of History and Biography* (1940), Vol.64, p.200.

36 Journal of the House of Commons, Vol. 62, 1806-07, 27 February 1807.

37 Willan, *River Navigation in England*, p.99.

38 W.E. Minchinton ed., *The Trade of Bristol in the Eighteenth Century* (Bristol, 1957), p.29.

39 Latimer, *Annals of Bristol*, Vol. 2, pp.161 & 164.

40 For a fuller account of the painting, see Brenda J. Buchanan, 'A View of the Jolly Sailor at Saltford Weir and Lock, near Bristol', *BIAS Journal* (Bristol Industrial Archaeological Society, 1993), Vol. 26, pp.20-1.

41 Robert W. Malcolmson, '"A Set of Ungovernable People": the Kingswood colliers in the eighteenth century', in John Brewer & John Styles eds., *An Ungovernable People: the English and their law in the seventeenth and eighteenth centuries* (1980), pp.104-5,114-6; Wood, *Description of Bath*, pp.368-70.

42 William Mathews, *The New History, Survey and Description of Bristol ...* (Bristol, 1794), p.33.

Acknowledgements

I should like to acknowledge the help received over the years from archivists at the Public Record Office, and the City Record Offices of Bath and Bristol; curators of the Victoria Art Gallery, Bath; and librarians at the Bath City Library and Bath University Library, especially the staff of the Inter-Library Loan and Graphics Departments at the last-named. And a special word of thanks to Angus Buchanan for sharing yet more field work in good spirits.

THE CLOTH INDUSTRY OF TWERTON
FROM THE 1780s TO THE 1820s

Nicholas von Behr

During the period of the early Industrial Revolution, the West of England region acquired an internationally-acknowledged reputation for the manufacture of superfine woollen cloth, a superior quality textile, woven with yarn made from the shorter, finer wool on the fleece, and specially finished to produce a smooth, felt-like surface. The region comprised two main topographical sub-regions: the Stroudwater, Cam and Little Avon valleys of southern Gloucestershire; and the Avon, Frome and Wylye valleys of western Wiltshire and north-east Somerset. The second of these sub-regions is commonly referred to as the Wiltshire-Somerset area, and within it lay the mills of the Bath area. During the period, wool textile manufacturing processes took place on mill sites at Batheaston, Bathwick and Twerton, or 'Twiverton' as it was then known. It is the sites on the south side of the two weirs across the River Avon at the last-named village, located about one-and-a-half miles to the west of Bath, which are the subject of this study (fig. 1).

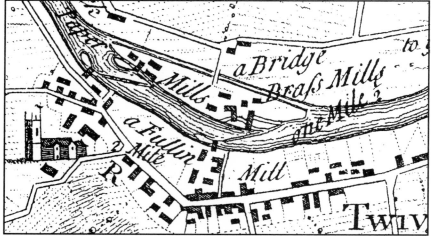

1. Map of Twerton mill sites in the eighteenth century. This section of the *Survey of Five Miles round the City of Bath* by Thomas Thorpe, 1742, shows the River Avon with its two weirs, the Twerton mills on the south bank, and the Weston mills on the island created by the Weston Navigation Cut.

The origins of cloth manufacturing at Twerton are inextricably linked with the River Avon. The very name of the village suggests the presence of two fords before Saxon times, and in 945AD there is the first mention of a weir. In the Domesday Book, four mills each worth 30 shillings rent are mentioned in two entries for 'Twertone', and subsequent records of Bath Abbey for the thirteenth and fourteenth centuries show that watermills at Twerton were being leased for grist milling. The Abbey was at that time involved in a thriving local woollen cloth manufacture, but there is no evidence to show that the Twerton mills were used for fulling the woven material – that is, subjecting the wet cloth to continuous hammering by water-powered stocks, making the threads shrink and thicken to produce a matted finish. By the late fifteenth century, however, two mills on the Twerton bank of the Avon were being used to full cloth, each containing two sets of stocks. The lower of the mills reverted to grist milling in the seventeenth century, long after the collapse of the original Bath cloth industry in the middle of the previous century, while the upper one continued fulling into the eighteenth century. In 1727, the completion of the Avon Navigation linking Bath to Bristol saw the creation of what would subsequently be called 'Dutch Island' on the north bank of the River Avon opposite Twerton. At around the same time, a new building was erected at the lower mill site, adjoining the original grist mill known as Chatterton's Mill, and used for paper manufacture.[1]

By the third decade of the eighteenth century, the upper mill on the Twerton bank of the Avon had come into the proprietorship of Isaac Sperin. Sperin proved to be a successful entrepreneur, starting with the manufacture of drugget (a coarse wool cloth, made from worsted yarn) and eventually producing serge, a popular, lighter and cheaper hybrid woollen cloth, made by weaving worsted with woollen yarn.[2] The success of his business is evidenced by a painting of Twerton Upper Mill dated February 1781, on which a written description refers to the fact that Isaac Sperin had 'made a fortune' – the occupier of the mill at that time was Samuel Heaven, a clothier from Gloucester, and James Lockstone, a serge maker, continued manufacturing in the 'fabrik' after Sperin's son.[3] In January 1787 an advertisement appeared in the *Bath Chronicle* for the sale of the mill together with its contents, 'now in the possession of Mr Samuel Heaven'.[4] Apart from the original fulling mill, the manufacturing premises also included a dyehouse, several large workshops, and a rack close for tentering the woven cloths by stretching them out to dry after fulling. More importantly, an undisclosed number of spinning jennies and a gig mill were put up for auction, the first direct reference to textile machinery used at Twerton.

2. Aerial view of Twerton Upper Mill site in 1930. Bamford, Cook & Company's original factory buildings dating from the late eighteenth century form a T-shape in the centre of the complex. (*Reproduced by courtesy of the Turner-Messer Twerton Archive*)

The spinning jenny, invented by James Hargreaves in 1764, was a hand-powered, multi-spindle machine designed to replace the traditional spinning wheel in the Lancashire cotton industry. Its use eventually spread to the neighbouring Yorkshire wool industry, and the first machines arrived in the West of England region at Shepton Mallet in 1776, causing a riot and their subsequent destruction.[5] Because of this adverse response, and the fact that the early jennies were not ideally suited to producing a fine woollen yarn, the machine did not take hold in the region until the late 1780s, when Twerton Upper Mill became one of the first recorded premises to operate them.[6] The gig mill, probably originating in Tudor times, was a large revolving drum fitted with teasels, used in place of manual labour to raise the nap of woven cloth before it was sheared. Where it was water-powered, which was probably the case at Twerton, it was usually connected by gearing to the fulling stocks.[7] Petitioners against its use in 1796 claimed that a 250-year old statute had made the machine illegal, though it seems more likely that this had been intended to prevent damage to finer cloths.[8]

Samuel Paul Bamford was in occupation at Twerton Upper Mill site by 1789, having probably come from the Devon area of the serge industry. This last supposition is supported by the fact that he seems to have returned there four years after his involvement with Twerton Upper Mill had come to an end: the records of the Bath and West Society, of which he was a member from 1793 to 1815, show that from 1806 onwards he was residing in Exeter.[9] Moreover, in 1815 he is recorded as leasing a serge factory with spinning machinery in Chudleigh.[10] The first local record of Bamford's name at Twerton is in the minutes of the parish vestry, where his signature is found with those who attended the meeting of 13 April 1789.[11] A covenant of January the following year between Bamford and Ebenezer Coombs, a clothier from Corsley in Wiltshire, refers to two mills which had been 'converted into and then used by the said Samuel Paul Bamford as a Worsted Mill', but gives no indication of when this happened.[12] The two original mills were the fulling mill and an adjoining china mill. It seems likely that the block referred to in 1802 as the 'Worsted Mill', whose dimensions were 106 by 32 feet, rising six storeys, was the newly-constructed building which replaced them.[13] The larger, adjoining 'Cloth-House or Mill' of 122 by 32 feet was probably built at a later date, and may have been occupied by James Clifford who was manufacturing woollen cloth at Twerton in 1796, and who, together with a John Cook from Trowbridge, became a partner of Bamford's by the turn of the century (fig. 2).[14]

The first clear evidence of textile machinery operated by Bamford is a letter written by him in February 1792 to Sir George Yonge, the War Secretary, requesting military protection for his mill against an imminent attack by a group of Wiltshire scribblers.[15] The reason for their planned act of violence was his recent introduction of a 'scribbling machine'. This piece of machinery, perfected by Richard Arkwright in 1775 for use in the cotton industry, was designed to replace the process of opening and mixing the raw wool by hand-held cards before spinning. With mechanization the process was separated into two parts: a scribbling machine opened up the raw wool, which was then placed in a carding machine, worked further, and converted into slivers ready for use on a spinning jenny. Both stages were usually powered by water, though occasionally by horse. The machinery had been introduced successfully into the West Riding from the late 1770s, but it was not until May 1791 that its presence was first recorded in the West of England region, causing a riot in Bradford-on-Avon and the destruction of the offending machine.[16] Bamford may have felt that the distance of Twerton from the main cloth towns of Wiltshire and Somerset, and the permanent presence of troops in the west of England, meant that he would be untroubled by such a violent response.[17] John Ford, a manufacturer of scribbling and carding machinery, had moved to Bath from Frome in December 1791, probably as a result of intimidation by cloth workers.[18] By April 1792 he had certainly supplied his machinery to William Abrahams, who was probably operating it on premises at the Bathwick Mill site, on the opposite side of the Avon from the city.[19] It is possible that Ford's move in some way contributed to the subsequent focus of hostility on the Bath area, though it seems that in this case the threat of violence against Twerton Upper Mill did not materialize.

The next reference to machinery at Twerton Upper Mill came a little over a year later in April 1793, in a further letter from Bamford to the War Secretary.[20] He began by stating that 'for some time past we have carried on a very extensive manufactory in spinning worked by machinery and lately have introduced several branches of the new invented patent machinery obtained by the Rev Edmund Cartwright of Duncaster [Doncaster] in Yorkshire'.[21] This last was a woolcombing machine, patented by Cartwright between 1790 and 1792, and designed to sort the longer wool staples before spinning into worsted yarn.[22] Bamford may have been one of the earliest purchasers of the machine, for having gone up north to see it for himself in December 1792, he promptly ordered one, which he had in operation at his factory by the following February.[23]

The threat of violence now came from the West of England woolcombers, and the response to Bamford's appeal for protection (his letter was endorsed by two Somerset magistrates) was more positive than previously, Yonge authorizing the dispatch of a troop of dragoons to Bath. Nonetheless, a year later petitions were sent to Parliament by woolcombers in Devon, Somerset and Wiltshire complaining of the 'invention and practice of a machine for combing of wool, which diminishes labour to an alarming degree'.[24] In the subsequent hearings before a House of Commons select committee, William Eales, a wool-comber from Plymouth who had worked at Bamford's factory, testified that the Twerton machine was powered by water. It seems to have run continuously, day and night, and of most significance to those listening, could 'clear out' 18 pounds of wool per hour, a size of output which Eales maintained could only be equalled by the best workers in 30 hours. Indeed, such was the machine's productivity, that Eales and most of his fellow woolcombers were soon laid off.[25]

At the end of 1797, Bamford's factory was again associated with the threat of anti-machinery violence. One night in December of that year, a group of 800 to 900 armed shearmen and sypathisers from the Wiltshire-Somerset area woollen towns gathered together. Some of their number having forcibly entered a workshop near Frome, in which they had discovered and destroyed shears belonging to the Twerton Upper Mill, they resolved to meet again the following Sunday to 'proceed to Twerton in order to hang up Bamford and two of his men, to burn down his works and those of Collicott and Co. on the opposite side of the river'.[26] It seems likely that the destroyed implements were being used in a number of shearing frames at the factory. These machines had been invented ten years before by John Harmer of Sheffield, in order to replace the manual shearing of raised cloth to give it a smooth finish, and had already been introduced into the West of England region of the woollen industry by the mid-1790s.[27] In the event, the plan was uncovered by a Bath magistrate, who drafted in soldiers to discourage an attack. A group of about 150 men did get as far as the cottage of one of the factory workers, but rapidly dispersed when a troop of cavalry was called in. The other main threat to the livelihood of the West of England shearmen was the gig mill, and as its use spread from Gloucestershire down to Wiltshire and Somerset, their increasing hostility was directed at those mills which operated the machinery. Influenced no doubt by the pace of mechanization at Twerton, where two gigs were probably in operation by that time, other mills in the Bath area also began to employ cloth-dressing machinery, attracting

3. An early water-powered gig mill (above) and shearing frame (below), the object of anti-machinery violence at Twerton at the turn of the eighteenth and nineteenth centuries. (*Abraham Rees, The Cyclopaedia (1802-19), courtesy of Bath Reference Library*)

custom from clothiers in Bradford-on-Avon, Trowbridge, Chippenham and Melksham.[28] Thus in April 1799, the proprietor of Batheaston Mill, John Bell, was threatened by the cloth workers of those towns, warning him not to use his gig mill, and to give his 'Brother Brown a Caution of this as hee will shear the same fate and Cook and Bamford Allso'.[29] 'Brother Brown' was Ebenezer Brown, Bell's brother-in-law, who by 1800 had moved his cloth manufactory from Bradford-on-Avon to the lower mill site at Twerton (see below), in which Bell eventually acquired a sharing interest.[30]

A contemporary description of Twerton Upper Mill during this busy period comes from a *History of Bath*, published in 1800, in which the author, the Reverend Richard Warner, describes 'some useful manufactures' in the neighbourhood of the city.[31] He specifically mentions the presence at 'Bamford, Cook & Co.' of 'curious machinery, consisting of many thousands of small wheels, worked by one large water-wheel', and was probably referring to a range of water-powered, worsted-spinning machines, including Richard Arkwright's waterframe originally patented in 1769.[32] According to Warner, manufacturing was carried out on the premises by 300 adult and 80 child employees. But the business evidently felt the effects of the trade depression of 1801-2, for it was declared bankrupt, and the machinery and premises were advertised for sale, firstly in February 1802, and subsequently in July.[33] Here at last is a detailed inventory of the factory, and what it reveals in terms of mechanization by that time is quite impressive: for worsted production there were 'washing, combing, regulating, drawing, roving, and spinning machines and frames'; for woollen manufacture, 'engines for opening wool, scribbling and carding machines, billies, jennies, reels, ... two gig-mills, ... eighteen patent shearing frames, shears and brushing-up machine'.[34] While the exact type of machine used is, in some cases, unclear from the description, it is worth making a brief examination of the new machinery mentioned.

William Partridge, in his 1823 account of woollen cloth manufacture, describes an 'apparatus' oblong in shape, occasionally made of sheet copper, which was perforated in the top half of its sides and, once filled with previously scoured wool, was placed in a flowing stream of water.[35] This may possibly be the type of wool-washing machine referred to in the 1802 inventory. The machines for 'regulating, drawing, roving' were all designed, as previously mentioned, to work on the same principle as Arkwright's waterframe, employing water-powered rollers to process slivers of wool to an increasing fineness. The machine for opening the raw wool was probably a willey, a cylindrical drum with spikes or teeth, similar in many ways to scribbling and carding machines.[36] The 'slubbing billy' linked the processes of carding and spinning after the introduction of the jenny, and was based on the same principles as the latter, imparting twist to the wool slivers to create slubbings ready for spinning. It was to become the subject of much concern during the early nineteenth century debates on the reform of child labour, because of the instances of cruelty inflicted on the 'pieceners', the young children whose job it was continuously to feed the machine with slivers of wool.[37] Finally, the brushing machine may at this time have been unique to Twerton Upper Mill in the whole of the West of England region. Partridge described it in 1823 as 'a machine, made similar to a gig-mill, only much smaller in the barrel, and having three or four rows of brushes on it', used to give an end-finish to the woollen cloth after shearing.[38]

Separate evidence of the extent of mechanization at Bamford's factory is provided by his recorded use of child apprentices from the very beginning of manufacturing. In August 1789, the Twerton parish vestry minutes record that he was granted the labour of two pauper children for almost two years' service at three shillings cost per week to the parish. Within a couple of months it was clear that Bamford had begun to take in apprentices from other parishes as well, for at another vestry meeting, from which he was absent, it was agreed that if he continued to do this, an application would be made to 'the Justices for Orders of removal unless they bring proper discharge from their Parish'.[39] Whatever the outcome of this resolution, four years later Bamford placed an advertisement in the regional press for 40 to 60 children aged nine and above (the woolcombing machines he had first installed in February of that year each required 11 children to feed them continuously with raw wool).[40] Moreover, in 1796 he responded to newspaper advertisements placed by the Exeter authorities for pauper children to work in factories. He duly received 40 to 50 boys and girls in May of that year, while James Clifford, presumably in the recently-built adjoining woollen cloth mill, received another 30 apprentices soon after.[41] Thus, by the time of Warner's tour of the factory in 1800, he would report that there were 80 children employed and boarded at the factory of Bamford, Cook & Co., all of whom were 'taken at the early age of eight or ten years from the neighbouring parish workhouses and regularly bound apprentices to the firm til the age of twenty-one'.[42]

It is possible to make some general conclusions about the regional significance of the factory at the start of the nineteenth century. Firstly, it is clear that the Twerton Upper Mill site was using the latest techniques in worsted and woollen manufacturing, and employing a large number of workers, a significant proportion of whom were children, as well as the machinery required to achieve this. Secondly, while Samuel Bamford was certainly prominent in introducing wool-preparing machinery to the south-west wool textile industry during the early 1790s, Bamford, Cook & Co. was a driving force behind the adoption of mechanized finishing processes in the Wiltshire-Somerset area during the later years of the decade. Finally, the Twerton Upper Mill operation compares well with that of the largest wool textile manufacturer at that time, Benjamin Gott, who had established a factory near Leeds in 1793.[43] For example, the total insurance value of Gott's premises, machinery and stock in 1797 was £6,000 – Bamford, Cook & Co's for the same year was £5,100, half of which covered machinery alone.[44] While Gott had more employees (about 1,000 in and out of the factory) and a large number of scribbling and carding machines, he was operating neither gig mills nor shearing frames to finish his superfine broadcloth, as he was prevented from doing so by his highly skilled workforce.[45]

At some time between September and December 1802, Francis Naish took over the freehold of Twerton Upper Mill and began operating his woollen cloth manufactory on its premises.[46] Naish was a Trowbridge clothier with a large trade in fancy waistcoatings, whose name had already been closely linked with new working methods and machinery in the 1790s. In 1791 he had advertised for twenty weavers to work in his large loomshop, as well as a foreman who understood carding machines.[47] The following year, Naish bought an isolated mill at nearby Littleton and rented it out for the operation of finishing machinery, including a gig mill and possibly shearing frames. He may also have been prominent in demanding wage reductions to cut the cost of finishing, a move which eventually incited the shearmen to go out on strike in the summer of 1802.[48] On 22 July of that year, following a number of outbreaks of violence, they destroyed Littleton mill at an estimated loss to Naish of £8,000. As a result, the Trowbridge clothiers conceded to all of the demands of their shearmen, but a fortnight later, following the arrest of one of Naish's workmen for his involvement in the Littleton attack, the clothier's house and workshops in town were burnt down.[49] There seems, therefore, every reason for his move to Twerton, given that it was suitably distant from the main cloth centres to allow him to rebuild his business undisturbed, and that it was already well-advanced in terms of mechanization.

A contemporary's view of Francis Naish's business at Twerton is found in a description of the West of England woollen industry in 1814:

At Twerton, near Bath, I saw looms in Naish's factory for making fine woollen cloth. These looms are fitted with an appliance which stretches the cloth during the weaving process. I saw several women weavers at work in this factory ... I saw some excellent mechanical shears for cutting cashmere cloth at Twerton. They each had four blades which are in a fixed position. The cloth was drawn length ways across the blades.[50]

This new type of shearing frame, which allowed the cloth to be sheared continuously from end to end, may possibly have been an early invention of Joseph Clissild Daniell, whose name would later be more closely associated with Charles Wilkins at Twerton.[51] The 'cashmere' referred to was cassimere, a fine, narrow woollen cloth which represented a significant proportion of Naish's manufacture.

When a list of the area's principal woollen cloth manufacturers was presented two years later as evidence before a Parliamentary Select Committee on child labour, its main omissions were Twerton Upper Mill, and Bridge Mill in Trowbridge, both of which not only contained large amounts of machinery but were also, or had recently been, closely linked to Francis Naish.[52] This may have been due to the fact that both factories were experiencing serious financial problems: by March 1817 all Naish's property was assigned to a commission of bankruptcy, while the new owners of his Trowbridge factory were to put it on the market in the following year.[53] When an advertisement for the auction of the Twerton Upper Mill site, including all the machinery Naish had accumulated, appeared in the local press in May 1818, the extent of mechanization was impressive, including as it did 30 scribbling and carding machines, 70 spinning jennies, 12 pairs of fulling stocks, six gig mills (of which two were 'nearly new, and upon the most approved principles') and 50 shearing frames.[54] The large number of spring looms, 160 in total, is interesting, as aside from those introduced in Gloucestershire, the West of England weavers were reluctant to embrace the flying shuttle which threatened to displace one in four of them.[55] Based on estimates of workers per machine, it seems that Naish probably had a similar, if not greater, number of employees as Bamford, Cook & Co. before him, and more importantly, this may have represented the largest factory workforce in the Wiltshire-Somerset area of the cloth industry at that time.[56]

Final evidence of the scale of manufacture at Naish's factory comes from Twerton local historian R.G. Naish (no relation) in 1938, quoting from an auctioneer's notebook of June 1822, then in his possession, which described the factory as being powered by two waterwheels of 90 horse power with a capacity 'equal to the consumption of 25 bags of wool and six bags of silk weekly'.[57] In May of 1822 the local press had featured an appeal for public donations to relieve the unemployed workers and their families as a result of the 'recent stoppage of all employment at the Manufactory of Mr Naish at Twerton', while an advertisement for the auction in June, which included the sale of 40 cottages built by Naish to house an expanding workforce, confirmed the 'extraordinary power' of the mills.[58] It seems therefore that manufacturing continued at the Twerton Upper Mill under Naish's name for five years after his bankruptcy, and it was only in May 1824 that he ceased to pay poor rates on it, ownership having by then been transferred to Charles Wilkins (see below).[59] In his answers to the Factory Commissioners' questionnaire in 1833, Wilkins mentioned the fact that Twerton Upper Mill had been enlarged around the year 1807, a further indication of the growth in the scale of manufacture under Francis Naish's proprietorship.[60]

In 1784, the lower mill site at Twerton came into the occupation of Matthias Taylor, a leather dresser, who subsequently leased out part of the premises as an edge-tool mill. Paper manufacturing had by then come to an end, while grist milling continued at the original Chatterton's Mill.[61] In 1799, Taylor offered his share in the property for sale, with newly-extended premises capable of conversion into 'any manufactory', and within a year this had been transferred to Ebenezer Brown, a clothier from Bradford-on-Avon.[62] A plan of the site of about ten years later shows that Brown seems to have converted the main premises into a woollen cloth factory, erecting a drying house on adjoining land, and continuing to lease out Chatterton's Mill as Taylor had done before him. A witness testifying before the Parliamentary Select Committee of 1803, which was considering the repeal of restrictive Tudor legislation on the woollen industry, said that as a tenterer at Brown's manufactory he had seen cloth 'very much damaged' by the gig mill in use there.[63] An indenture dated 11 November 1807 records the lease of the freehold of all 'that mill or those mills now in the possession of them the said Ebenezer Brown and Charles Wilkins and wherein they now carry out the trade or business of clothiers with a machine therein called a gig and five pair of stocks for fulling or milling of cloth', for a 21-year period by Brown to Wilkins, at an annual rent of £400.[64] This is the first evidence of

4. Twerton Lower Mill site in the late nineteenth century, showing the original five-storey factory erected by Ebenezer Brown, c.1800, in the centre. (*Reproduced by courtesy of the Turner-Messer Twerton Archive*)

Charles Wilkins' involvement in cloth manufacturing at Twerton. In the same year, Ebenezer Brown leased another mill in Bradford, in which he installed a 14 horse-power steam engine, the first clear proof that one of the Twerton manufacturers was using steam power.[65] He soon experienced financial difficulties, and by July 1809 he had been declared bankrupt. Two months later the total amount owed to Wilkins, who had paid off some off Brown's debts, was more than £2,000. It seems that over the following years, Wilkins negotiated with Brown's numerous creditors for the purchase of their shares in the Twerton Lower Mill property.[66]

The best indication of the scale of manufacturing at the Twerton Lower Mill site at this time comes from the minutes of the 1816 'Select Committee on the State of the Children Employed in the Manufactories of the United Kingdom'. A solicitor from Bradford-on-Avon, John Bush, provided the committee with details of the number and age of employees at what he termed 'the principle woollen manufactories in Wilts, and part of Somerset', including his own family's not insignificant business.[67] The list covered thirty-two other manufacturers, half of whom were located in the main cloth areas of Bradford-on-Avon and Trowbridge – the rest were to be found within a ten-mile circumference. When ranked in order of the number of factory workers employed, the largest concern was Saunders, Fanner & Co. of Bradford, operating from two separate premises with 321 employees, while the smallest belonged to John & Thomas Clark of Trowbridge, with only 35 employees. 'Messrs Charles Wilkins & Co., Tiverton' (a misprint) came seventh in rank with 167 employees. Of these, 111 were adults and the remaining 56 children, including 13 under ten years of age. It was therefore a sizeable operation by regional comparison, though certainly not as large as Francis Naish's factory at Twerton Upper Mill which had been omitted from the list (see above). In the following year the factory was enlarged by Wilkins, and this may have included the installation of a steam engine – one was certainly operating at Twerton Lower Mill in 1819.[68] By 1824 he also occupied the larger upper mill site, and during the following decades his business leadership was to place Twerton at the forefront of the superfine woollen cloth industry in both the West of England and Britain as a whole, during the nineteenth century.[69]

How did the Twerton factories compare with other wool textile manufacturing premises in the Wiltshire-Somerset area during the early part of the Industrial Revolution? Using Kenneth Rogers' comprehensive

5. View of Twerton in the first half of the nineteenth century, depicting the upper and lower mill sites at the height of their expansion under Charles Wilkins. (From J.C. Bourne, History and Description of the Great Western Railway (1846), courtesy of R.A. Buchanan)

survey of eighteenth- and nineteenth-century woollen mills, it can be shown that there were only a handful of comparable workshop or factory premises in the region at the start of the 1790s.[70] The earliest to be erected, in 1785, was John Anstie's four-storey workshop building in Devizes, which probably contained horse-powered carding machinery and hand-powered jennies; its total floor area was an impressive 8,000 sqare feet.[71] Bamford's worsted mill was completed at about the same time as four other newly-built or converted water-powered wool textile mills, at Westbury Leigh, Malmesbury, Quemerford and Avoncliff, roughly around the year 1790.[72] The significant difference between these, and indeed Anstie's workshop, and the Twerton Upper Mill, was the fact that while the former were of four to five storeys and had total working areas of between 5,600 and 7,600 square feet, the latter was six storeys high and had a total floor area of over 20,000 square feet.[73] By the turn of the century, only three other premises had been built or converted on a scale similar to Bamford's original building: at Christian Malford in 1795; at Weston Lower Mill, on the opposite side of the Avon in the mid-1790s (see Appendix); and at Staverton, near Bradford-on-Avon, in 1800.[74] The last of these had seven storeys and a working area of 28,800 square feet, and was thus the first factory to exceed the size of Bamford's worsted mill. However, the larger, adjoining woollen cloth mill had been built by then, which brought the complete floor area of the two main buildings belonging to Bamford, Cook & Co., to almost 44,000 square feet.[75] An impression of their combined size can be obtained from the aerial photograph taken in 1930, where they are seen forming the central part of the T-shaped factory (fig. 2). By that time, the premises at the Twerton Upper and Lower Mill sites had undergone expansion and rebuilding, firstly under Francis Naish and Ebenezer Brown, then by Charles Wilkins, from the 1820s to the 1840s, and subsequently under the family dynasty of the Carrs into the twentieth century.

Under these enterprising manufacturers the two eighteenth-century mill sites on the south bank of the River Avon at Twerton village were transformed into factory premises, where by the mid-1820s the foundations for the emergence of an internationally-renowned superfine cloth industry had been laid. The parish of Twerton became a growing industrial suburb which was absorbed into the city of Bath in the early twentieth century. Cloth manufacturing continued at Twerton until its demise in the 1950s, in the face of competition from Yorkshire and abroad.

Appendix: The Weston Mills

By the early eighteenth century, the upper part of the Weston mills was being used for the manufacture of brassware, having been acquired, in 1711, by the Bristol Brass Company.[76] We know from Warner's description of Twerton in 1800 that a Mr Collicott was running a cloth factory at what was certainly the lower mill site.[77] These premises had been the proposed target of the same group of wool workers who, as previously mentioned, had in December 1797 resolved to destroy Twerton Upper Mill. It is clear therefore that Collicott was operating textile machinery in much the same way as Bamford, Cook & Co., though on a smaller scale, and limited to the production of a superfine woollen broadcloth. Indeed, it was an enterprise that outlasted those of both Bamford and his successor Francis Naish, until Collicott's eventual bankruptcy in 1825.[78] The best available evidence of the size of his business comes from an 1829 advertisement in the local press, for the sale by auction of the mill and other property belonging to the 'mortgagee in trust' – unfortunately, no details are given of machinery.[79] The 'clothing mill manufactory', presumably the original built by Collicott in the mid-1790s, had dimensions of 68 by 46 feet, rising six storeys, giving a total floor area of almost 19,000 square feet, and making it the third largest factory in the Wiltshire-Somerset area before 1800. It was powered by two water wheels and could produce an output of twenty broadcloths per week. It is interesting to note that, according to Warner, Collicott also owned the upper mill site on the Weston side of the Avon, which continued to manufacture brass utensils as it had done since the early eighteenth century, as well as an adjoining mill for 'beating out bars of steel' – thus forming a small industrial complex.[80] These two separate premises were sold to Francis Naish at some time before his bankruptcy, and were converted by him to logwood and flour mills.[81]

Notes

1   Sources used for this paragraph are: M. Chapman, 'The Historical Background to Industrial Twerton', unpublished folio written for the Bath Industrial Heritage Centre (BIHC); W.S. Shaw, 'Notes on the History of Twerton', *Proceedings of the Bath Natural History and Antiquarian Field Club*, Vol. 2 (1870-2), pp.271-81; J. Day, *Bristol Brass: the History of the Industry* (Newton Abbot, 1973), pp.64-5; and title deeds to the Twerton Upper and Lower Mills, records of which are held at the BIHC.

2   R.G. Naish, *Bath & Wiltshire Herald & Gazette*, 16 December 1937.

3   *Ibid.*, 20 December 1937. A colour slide of the painting is held at the BIHC as part of the Turner-Messer Archive on the history of Twerton.
4   *Bath Chronicle*, 4 January 1787.
5   K.G. Ponting, *The Woollen Industry of South West England* (Bath, 1971), p.37; K.H. Rogers, *Wiltshire and Somerset Woollen Mills* (Edington, 1976), pp.19, 169.
6   J. de L. Mann, *The Cloth Industry in the West of England from 1640 to 1880* (Oxford, 1971), pp.123-9.
7   *Ibid.*, pp.141-2, 300.
8   A. Randall, 'The Shearmen and the Wiltshire Outrages of 1802: Trade Unionism and Industrial Violence', *Social History*, Vol. 7 (1982), p.287.
9   University of Bath, Royal Bath and West Society Archives, annual reports of 1793 to 1815.
10 Devon Record Office (DRO), 924B/B8/26, lease 17 November 1815.
11 Somerset Record Office (SRO), D/P/Twn–9/1/1, Twerton Vestry Minutes 1780-1848, 13 April 1789.
12 Wiltshire Record Office (WRO), 628, 16/17, covenant 7 February 1790. An 'Ebenezer Sperrin Coombs' was manufacturing silk at Corsley in the early nineteenth century, a fact which suggests that the Coombs and Sperin families may have been related by marriage. Rogers (1976), p.200.
13 *Bath Journal*, 1 December 1802.
14 *Ibid.*; DRO, No. 13 ECA, Corporation of the Poor Court Book 1766-1801, 20 June 1796; *London Gazette*, May 1799, p.507.
15 Public Record Office (PRO), WO 1/1054, letter from Bamford to Yonge, 5 February 1792. Yonge, Member of Parliament for Honiton in Devon since 1754 and War Secretary from 1782-1794, had, together with Sir John Duntze, built a new serge factory at Ottery St Mary in the early 1790s, in an attempt to revive the industry in that area. *Dictionary of National Biography*, Vol. XXI (1949-50), p.1239.
16 Mann (1971), pp.129-30; D.T. Jenkins, *The West Riding Wool Textile Industry* (Edington, 1975), p.117.
17 A. Randall, *Before the Luddites – Custom, Community and Machinery in the English Woollen Industry* (Cambridge, 1991), pp.75-80, 105.
18 Rogers (1976), pp.22, 168.
19 *Bath Herald & General Advertiser*, 28 April 1792.
20 PRO, WO 1/1056, letter from Bamford to Yonge, 26 April 1793.
21 *Ibid.*
22 J. James, *History of the Worsted Manufacture in England* (1857, reprint 1968), pp.565-6.
23 Journals of the House of Commons (JHC), Vol. XLIV, 13 March 1794.
24 Quoted in H.C. Oram, 'The Industrial Revolution and the Textile Industries of Somerset 1750-1870', unpublished MA thesis, University of Bristol (1930), Appendix A.
25 JHC, Vol. XLIV, 13 March 1794.
26 PRO, HO 42/41, letter from Bowen to Portland, 20 December 1797. Collicott was operating a cloth factory at the Weston Lower Mill site (see Appendix).
27 Mann (1971), pp.134, 149-50.
28 *Ibid.*, p.142; Randall (1991), pp.151-93.

29   *London Gazette,* May 1799, p.507; Randall (1991), p.153.
30   BIHC, Twerton Lower Mill deeds, mortgage 8 October 1804.
31   R. Warner, *History of Bath* (Bath, 1801), p.215.
32   *Ibid.;* Mann (1971), p.134.
33   *Bath Journal,* 1 February 1802; *Bath Chronicle,* 8 July 1802; Randall (1991), pp.197-8.
34   *Bath Chronicle,* 8 July 1802.
35   W.Partridge, *A practical treatise on dying of woollen, cotton, and skein silk with the manufacture of broadcloth and cassimere including the most improved methods in the West of England* (1823, reprint Edington 1973), p.30.
36   Mann (1971), p.280.
37   *Ibid.,* p.288.
38   *Ibid.,* p.300; Partridge (1973), p.84.
39   SRO, D/P/Twn – 9/1/1, Twerton Vestry Minutes 1780-1848, 2 August & 5 November 1789.
40   K. Rogers, *Warp and Weft* (Buckingham, 1986), p.74; JHC, Vol. XLIV, 13 March 1794.
41   DRO, No. 13 ECA, Corporation of the Poor Court Book, 1766-1801, 12 May & 20 June 1796.
42   Warner (1801), p.216.
43   H. Heaton, 'Benjamin Gott and the Industrial Revolution in Yorkshire', *Economic History Review,* Vol. 3 (1930-1), pp.51, 55.
44   Jenkins (1975), pp.97-9; Rogers (1986), p.74.
45   Heaton (1930-1), pp.53-4, 58.
46   SRO, D/P/Twn – 9/1/1, Twerton Vestry Minutes, 1780-1848, 17 September & 30 December 1802.
47   Rogers (1976), p.22.
48   Randall (1982), p.291.
49   Randall (1991), pp.162-3.
50   Reproduced in Ponting (1971), p.158.
51   Rogers (1976), p.23; Mann (1971), p.303.
52   British Parliamentary Papers (BPP), 1816, Vol III, 'Select Committee on the State of the Children Employed in the Manufactories of the United Kingdom', pp.308-9.
53   SRO, DD/X/WBB, 17/2/1, assignment of 20 March 1817; Rogers (1976), p.136.
54   *Bath & Cheltenham Gazette,* 13 May 1818.
55   Mann (1971), pp.139-41; Randall (1991), pp.98, 100, 189.
56   N. von Behr, 'The Wool Textile Industry of Twerton: a study in the development of factory manufacturing during the Industrial Revolution', unpublished MSc. project report, University of Bath (1995), p.22 & Appendix I.
57   R.G. Naish, *Bath & Wiltshire Herald & Gazette,* 19 & 22 August 1938.
58   *Bath Journal,* 20 May 1822 & 3 June 1822.
59   Bath Record Office, Twerton Poor Rates, 6 May 1824.
60   BPP, 1834, Vol. XX, 'Supplementary Report of the Central Board of Factory Commissioners, Pt. II', p.54.

61 BIHC, Twerton Lower Mill deeds, reversion 25 March 1784 & conveyance 29 September 1801.
62 *Bath Chronicle*, 21 March 1799; BIHC, Twerton Lower Mill deeds, assignment 29 January 1800.
63 BPP, 1802/3, Vol. VII, 'Minutes of Evidence taken before the Select Committee on the Woollen Clothier's Petition', pp.118-25.
64 BIHC, Twerton Lower Mill deeds, lease of 11 November 1807.
65 Rogers (1976), pp.161-2, 1698.
66 SRO, DD/OB, 21, abstract of title deeds to Twerton Lower Mill, 1837.
67 BPP, 1816, Vol. III, *op. cit.*, pp.308-9.
68 BPP, 1834, Vol. XX, *op. cit.*, p.54.
69 BIHC, Twerton Upper Mill deeds, mortgage of 24 April 1824.
70 Rogers (1976), pp.45-6.
71 *Ibid.*, pp.30, 105.
72 *Ibid.*, pp. 72-3, 84-5, 164-5, 218-9.
73 *Bath Chronicle*, 8 July 1802.
74 Rogers (1976), pp.75, 96-104; *Bath Chronicle*, 23 July 1829. It is difficult to estimate the total floor area of Ebenezer Brown's factory at the Twerton Lower Mill site.
75 *Bath Chronicle*, 8 July 1802.
76 Day (1973), p.64, supplemented by the author's notes from a public lecture given by Joan Day at Bath University in March 1995.
77 Warner (1801), p.217.
78 Mann (1971), p.172.
79 *Bath Chronicle*, 23 July 1829.
80 Warner (1801), p.217.
81 *Bath Journal*, 3 June 1822.

Acknowledgements

I would like to thank the following for their help and advice in the completion of this study: Angus Buchanan, Mike Chapman, Colin Johnston, the staff of the Bath Reference Library, Devon Record Office, Somerset Record Office and Wiltshire Record Office. Particular thanks go to Stuart Burroughs, curator of the Bath Industrial Heritage Centre, who not only started me on the research, but has been continuously involved since its inception.

BATH & THE
'BATH AND WEST OF ENGLAND SOCIETY',
1777-1851

Helena L.H. Lim

In the autumn of 1777, twenty-two gentlemen met in the city of Bath to form a society 'for the encouragement of Agriculture, Manufactures, Commerce and the Fine Arts' in the counties of Somerset, Wiltshire, Gloucester, Dorset, and the City and County of Bristol. It was known simply as 'The Society' or the 'Bath Society' since their meetings were held in Bath. In 1790, the title of the Society was altered to 'The Bath and West of England Society', on account of its well-established character and the widely-extended residences of its subscribers. A Royal Charter was granted in 1976.

From its inception, the Society operated from the city of Bath. Its meetings, activities and headquarters were based in Bath, and a significant proportion of its members were drawn from the city. This tie was to remain unbroken until the early 1850s when the Society began to hold its annual meeting, combined with an agricultural show, on a peripatetic basis throughout south-western England. The first seventy-four years of the Society's existence seem naturally to divide into three distinct periods. The first, from the late 1770s to the beginning of the nineteenth century, was one of great enthusiasm and drive. The second, from the 1820s to the 1840s, was a period of fluctuating success. The third, from the 1850s onwards, saw a change in the Society's direction in accordance with changed circumstances. All the while, the principal aim of improving agriculture remained in sight.

This paper will concentrate on the general development and activities of the Society during the first two periods, that is, the years between 1777 and 1851, when it was based in Bath. It will highlight the close ties between the Society and the city and inhabitants of Bath.

Background

The foundation of the Bath and West in 1777 can be understood with reference to more general trends and developments leading up to that date.

By the 1750s, England had enjoyed her years of peace and prosperity under Sir Robert Walpole, despite the uncertainty aroused by the 'South Sea Bubble', yet retaining her zeal for commercial enterprise.[1] The more far-sighted and public-spirited endeavoured to raise the productive powers of the nation, and societies for the promotion of agriculture in England and Wales began to emerge during the second half of the eighteenth century. Although the Royal Society, founded in 1660, had given attention to agriculture in its early years, its interest in practical subjects waned after its reorganization in 1690 so that it became essentially an academic body.[2] But positive steps were already being taken in Ireland and Scotland to encourage agricultural innovation and improvement. 'The Honourable Society of Improvers in the Knowledge of Agriculture in Scotland' was established in 1723, with its headquarters in Edinburgh. The Royal Dublin Society, founded under the title of the 'Dublin Society for Improving Husbandry, Manufactures and other Useful Arts', soon followed in 1731. 'The Society for the Encouragement of Arts, Manufacture and Commerce', generally known as the Society of Arts, was founded in London in 1754. The improvement of agriculture was one of its prime objectives well into the nineteenth century. Its *modus operandi* was the premium system, a novel way of stimulating innovation and invention by offering prizes and awards for new ideas, methods, or machinery. The premium system was seen as a plausible means of exciting a spirit of enquiry and innovation, as well as a way of encouraging adoption of the new techniques and technologies.

The foundation of the Society of Arts gave rise to many local imitators, one of the earliest being the Brecknockshire Society, founded in 1755 by Charles Powell, a Welsh philanthropist who took direct advice from the national society on its formation.[3] Similar local societies established during the second half of the eighteenth century took their inspiration from the Society of Arts but were independent of it. Much of their time was taken up with local affairs, but there were also discussions of new methods and ideas in agriculture. At this time, when knowledge of agricultural science and technique was growing rapidly, the foremost duty of the landlord was the care and improvement of his estate and the encouragement of better farming by his tenants. Thus, the problem of educating the ordinary farmer occupied the minds of the improving landlords. These agricultural societies provided a means by which to break down the resistance to innovation always to be found in the countryside.

The eighteenth-century agricultural societies typically consisted of gatherings of landowners and farmers to discuss new methods of husbandry and livestock improvement, new systems of farming and new crops. Coke of Holkham was prominent in this kind of activity and his 'Coke's Clippings' became large gatherings, attracting farmers and landowners from far and wide. There were also the famous sheep shearings of the Duke of Bedford at Woburn. Lord Somerville, a West Country nobleman, began holding a little annual show in London where he offered prizes for sheep, cattle and some improved implements, and demonstrated his own innovations in ploughs and carts. However, this group was not typical of the landed interest. It was with obvious justification that leading agricultural writers constantly complained of the indifference of the large landowners to the new husbandry. The majority of estates were cultivated conventionally and landowners tended to be more interested in securing efficient tenants than in experimenting with innovative techniques. This is where the agricultural societies stepped in and tried to arouse interest in the possibility of combining efficient tenants with both profit and increased rent. Their blueprint for success was the premium system. Premiums were sometimes offered for innovations but were more typically offered for excellence of stock or crops. It was also customary to offer premiums to agricultural workers for skill in agricultural operations such as ploughing, and to those who had successfully brought up large families without recourse to charity or poor relief.[4]

'The Bath and West' in Bath

The idea of an agricultural society based in Bath was the brain-child of Edmund Rack. The city of Bath in the late eighteenth century seems a most unlikely birthplace for an agricultural society. It was the Bath of Beau Nash, Ralph Allen and Jane Austen. In other words, the rank and fashion seemed more interested in dress and pleasure than in ploughs and turnips. Rack was born in 1735, in Attleborough, Norfolk, to Quaker parents. A draper by trade, he had also cultivated a taste for literature. During his earlier life in Norfolk, he had become very interested in agriculture and, in particular, the application of modern methods to farming. A knowledge of arithmetic appears to have been Rack's highest educational attainment, and for a while he was apprenticed to a general shopkeeper in Wymondham. At the close of his apprenticeship he moved to Essex, became a shopkeeper at Bardfield and married a Miss Agnes Smith. His business ambitions appear to have been limited to making enough money to allow him a pleasant life and an early retirement. He eventually retired in 1775, at the age of 40, and moved from Bardfield to Bath where he could pursue his literary ambitions.

At Bath, Rack was welcomed into the local literary circle which included Lady Miller's poetical revels in Batheaston and Mrs Catherine Macaulay's coterie at Alfred House.[5] Richard Cruttwell, the printer and publisher, also enlisted Rack's services for the *Farmer's Journal* and the *Bath Chronicle*. Rack was struck by the poor standard of farming practice in the west country and wrote a series of articles on the agriculture of the district. He recognized that the superiority of Norfolk agriculture was due to the fostering care of an agri-

1. Portrait of Edmund Rack from *The Agricultural Gazette*, June 1877

cultural society. Knowing the important part played by the Norfolk Agricultural Society in arousing interest in better farming and ensuring that it led to actual improvement, Rack came to the conclusion that a similar institution would be beneficial for the western counties. He wrote to the local press pointing out that it was in the interest of the farmer, the landowner and the nation in general that the agricultural resources of the country should be increased. He reported that it was the practice of the agricultural societies in London, Norwich and York, to give pecuniary and honorary rewards to the 'diligent and ingenious who have excelled in the various departments of husbandry, in useful manufactures, and in the most curious specimens of art',[6] and declared his intention to set up such a society, based in Bath, for the dissemination of the latest ideas in agriculture. Rack envisaged a society of broadly cultured people who would share his wish to advance the welfare of mankind, an admirable and thoroughly eighteenth-century ambition. The press proved considerably sympathetic and the following advertisement soon appeared in several local newspapers, including the *Bath Chronicle*:

AGRICULTURAL SOCIETY

To the Nobility and Gentry in the Counties of Somerset, Gloucester, Wilts and Dorset in general, and the Cities of Bath and Bristol in particular.

Bath; Aug. 26, 1777

A proposition having been made for the institution of a Society in this City for the encouragement of Agriculture, Planting, Manufactures, Commerce and the Fine Arts, the Nobility and Gentry are hereby respectfully informed that a Meeting will be held at York House, on Monday, the 8th of September, at Eleven o'clock in the forenoon, to take the affair under consideration. And that the plans on which Societies of this kind in London, Norwich, Manchester, &c., are founded, with some other necessary particulars, will then and there be produced; in order that a general plan may be formed for establishing a Society here on a proper foundation, and a subscription opened for carrying it on with a spirit becoming the dignity of so honourable an institution, and its great importance to the community.

As this institution is intended for the benefit for all the above-named counties, it is humbly requested that the public-spirited gentlemen residing therein will generally honour it with their countenance and protection.[7]

Several gentlemen responded to this invitation and met at York House where the Society was formed. In the minutes of the inaugural meeting are the names of those present that day. They included:

John Ford Esqr in the Chair	Phillip Stephens, Esq
Revd Dr Wilson	Paul Newman, Esq
Revd Mr Ford	Mr John Newman
Dr Wm Falconer	Willm Street, Esq
Dr Patrick Henley	Mr Symons, Surgeon
Wm Brereton, Esq	Mr Crutwell, Surgeon
Mr Saml Virgin	Mr Arden
Mr Richard Crutwell	Mr Wm Matthews
Mr Foster, Apothecary	Mr Parsons
Mr Cam Gyde	Mr Edm Rack
Mr Benj Axford	Mr Bull[8]

The founder-members were chiefly local professional men and included amongst them two clergymen, four doctors, an apothecary, a printer and publisher, but no farmer. Dr Falconer, being a Fellow of the Royal Society, was certainly the most distinguished of the founder-members.[9] He was the author of numerous books on medicine, science, religion, politics and classics. He settled in Bath after retiring from practice in London, and became Physician to the General Hospital. He lived in the Circus and remained an active member of the Society till his death in 1824. Despite the diverse professions of the founder-members of the Bath and West, they were held together by their patriotic fervour and their belief that they could improve the condition of agriculture in the western counties. This belief is reiterated in the following paragraph from George Winter's book of 1787, *A New and Compendious System of Husbandry:*

> Farmers may be possessed of great natural abilities and knowledge in the common mode of their ancestors; but every farmer is not a scholar, mechanic, chemist, or philosopher. Their knowledge, and the methods they pursue in general, extend no further than that of their predecessors, or the custom of the country where they reside. Any discoveries made by them are reserved to themselves, and themselves only benefit by it; but men of ingenuous and liberal dispositions, no sooner make discoveries, than they are communicated to the public.[10]

The first general meeting was held on 13 November 1777. It was attended by thirty-four people, and the Earl of Ilchester was elected President. In addition twelve vice-presidents were also elected. At this meeting, the aims, rules and orders of the Society were set out. The principal objectives were: to encourage what was broadly termed as 'industry'; to provide a channel for the exchange and dissemination of information; to carry out and publicize experiments in those areas most needing it; and to improve all aspects of husbandry through the award of premiums. These premiums were to be funded by the subscriptions and donations of public-spirited people. The annual subscription was fixed at 'not less than One Guinea' and the charge for life membership was 12 guineas.[11] It was also decided that Rack was to be paid 50 guineas a year as Secretary of the Society 'till the Society shall be better able to increase that sum'. The amount was increased to £70 in 1786. They also allowed him £30 a year for the use of rooms in his house at 5 St James's Parade.[12]

By the end of 1778, the Bath and West had 300 ordinary members and 54 honorary and consulting members. Among this latter group were such distinguished names as Arthur Young the agriculturalist, Joseph Priestley the chemist, and Thomas Curtis the botanist. Young was a frequent correspondent and contributor to the Society's journal. Curtis was later to become a vice-president of the Society till his death in 1784. Priestley was also to become a vice-president of the Society in 1778, and sat on the Committee of Correspondence and Enquiry in 1780.[13] Later, the honorary members of the Society were to include Sir Humphrey Davy, the man who first isolated sodium and potassium, and more surprisingly, Teyoninhok Arawen, a Mohawk chief who was very well disposed towards the Society.[14] There appears to be a wide overlap between the Society's early membership lists and the subscribers to the volume of poems, essay and letters which Rack published in 1781.[15] Among the 483 subscribers to the poems were Thomas Coke of Holkham, Arthur Young, William Herschel and the Duke of Marlborough. Many of the same people, distinguished or undistinguished, were persuaded to support the new Bath Society. Richard Cruttwell, the local printer who was present at the Society's inaugural meeting, printed and published both Rack's literary works and the Society's journal. A further link between Rack's agricultural and literary careers was that the chairman of the Society's first general meeting was Sir John Miller, the husband of Lady Miller.[16]

The Society immediately set to work on the basis established at its first general meeting – the plan being to use premiums as a means of encouragement and to raise a public fund to finance them. By the end of 1777, some £350 had been subscribed. The first premium list, agreed that December, was divided into three separate classes and seventy-six premiums were offered altogether. The subjects covered were very broad and varied from cultivating turnips and beans to studying epilepsy in pigs, from planting apple trees to introducing the manufacture of black silk lace and the invention of a machine for sowing carrot seed.[17] The Secretary was ordered to have 1,000 copies of the premium list printed. Every member was entitled to one and the rest were to go on sale. Fifty copies were to be sent to booksellers in each of the four counties.

New premiums were offered and duly announced at the beginning of every year in the Society's premium books. The premium lists were remarkably elaborate and they were most thoroughly organized. For example, the 1801 premium list occupied 45 pages of text and a total of 198 premiums were offered. The supervision of these activities was left to three specialist committees. These committees dealt with agriculture and planting, manufactures and commerce, and mechanics and useful arts. Their main tasks were to decide on the premiums which should be

2. 'The Prize Ox of the Bath and West of England Society, 1803. Weight Ten H[undred ?], Rough Fat eight score and upwards, Fed on Grass and Hay only, Bred and grazed by Mr Hall of Leigh Court, Somersetshire.' *(Reproduced by courtesy of Bath Reference Library, Hunt Collection)*

offered and awarded. These decisions were then presented to the annual meeting for final approval. It is interesting to note that the premiums offered in any one class serve as a general indicator of what the Society considered to be of immediate relevance to the region at any given time. For example, ploughs and trials of ploughs took up a lot of the Society's attention in the early days. However, drainage was the Society's main campaign by the 1840s. It was hoped that premiums would give a tremendous stimulus to agricultural advance. In the first twenty-five years of the Society's existence, some £2,070 was expended on them.

In June 1778, the Committee of Correspondence and Enquiry decided that a general knowledge of the best modes of practice in all the different parts of the country was essential to the success of their scheme. This is because they knew that farmers preferred practical examples to theoretical principles. Accordingly, they drew up a list of questions on which they wanted information and sent these off to the high sheriff of each county, requesting that suitably qualified persons be asked to answer the queries and return them to the Secretary. As a consequence they received a curious assortment of useful practical knowledge and superstitious notions.[18]

In 1779, the Society decided to acquire some land for the purpose of conducting experiments in agriculture.[19] By the spring of 1780, a site had been found and approved by Edmund Rack. Ten acres were taken over at Weston, on the outskirts of Bath, on the farm of one of the Society's members, Mr Bettel.[20] At this experimental farm, trials of various kinds were carried out by Mr Bettel on behalf of the Society, under the supervision of an Experimental Committee. This scheme eventually petered out after about ten years due to defective management and disagreement among the parties involved. Nevertheless, the farm which the Society operated at Weston was the very first experimental farm in Britain, and a worthy predecessor to Woburn and Rothamstead.

The first volume of *Letters and Papers* appeared in 1780. This included the selected reports, essays and letters which the Society had received from its correspondents and from competitors for premiums. Every subscribing member was entitled to a copy of this journal and the rest were sold at bookshops in London and the four counties for a small price. This was one of the earliest publications of its kind in the country. However, it appeared irregularly and terminated with Volume 15 in 1829. A second series was launched in 1853, and there were six series altogether.

Implements and machines, or models and drawings of them, were left at the Society's Rooms for the inspection of gentlemen and farmers. These were sent by the members, competitors for premiums, or purchased. As early as 1780, the exhibition of Mr Blancher's drill plough at the Society's

3. Mr Boswell's Norfolk Plough. One of the early illustrations of agricultural implements featured in the Society's *Letters and Papers* (Vol. 2, 1782, facing p.356). These often included elaborate descriptions of how the implements worked. A model of George Boswell's plough was left in the Society's Model Room for inspection .

Rooms was announced in the journal. Furthermore, it had been 'tried by our Agricultural Committee, in a field, and found to deliver the grain with great exactness and regularity, quite to the satisfaction of the Gentlemen Farmers who attended the experiment'.[21] It was hoped that this collection would provide for the diffusion of new inventions in the west country.

At the annual meeting of 1786, it was decided that a public trial of ploughs should be conducted:

> It being universally acknowledged that in the whole circle of agricultural practice there is nothing so interesting to the Farmer than to plow cheap & well, It is directed that fair Comparative Tryals shall be made in March next both on light & Heavy soils near Bath, with the various Ploughs generally used in the Western Counties against the Double share Norfolk, Essex, and other improved ploughs introduced by the Society.[22]

In order to induce farmers to participate, three premiums amounting to 12 guineas in total were offered for the three ploughs which performed the best. There were also rewards for ploughmen. Notice of this match was advertized in the local papers and the date set for 29 March 1787. Competitors were to be allowed to use whichever plough they chose. A Committee of Farmers was chosen to determine the comparative merits of the several ploughs used. However, the match did not take place as planned because of the death of Edmund Rack that February. At an extra general meeting, William Matthews was elected the new Secretary. Matthews, like Rack, was a Quaker, the son of an Oxfordshire shoemaker. He had settled in Bath in 1777, first setting up a brewery, then a coal yard, and then a seed and agricultural implement business which he ran from the Society's Rooms in Hetling House, now Abbey Church House (fig. 4).[23]

The first ploughing match finally took place in March 1788 on Barrack's Farm, Wells Road, Bath. There were six competitors and John Billingsley won the first prize with a double coulter plough, drawn by six oxen.[24] This is considered to be one of the first competitions of its kind in this or any other county. Subsequent matches were held at least once, and sometimes up to four times, a year. Different types of ploughs were tested, such as the double-furrow and the single-furrow ploughs, because although ploughs were meant to perform essentially the same task, they possessed regional differences in construction and design which made them particularly suited to the area from which they originated. Even the

4. Hetling House, 1847. This is the earliest surviving photograph of Hetling House. It was the Society's first headquarters and it is just possible to make out the 'Agricultural Society' sign above the first-floor windows. (*Bath Reference Library, E7/300*)

same 'type' of plough could have many variants in mouldboards and shares. For example, the double-furrow plough was very suitable for working light lands. The utility of these ploughing matches was that they demonstrated the most suitable ploughs for the west country.

In 1787, the Society had 266 ordinary members and 55 honorary and corresponding members. Forty-six of the ordinary members had a Bath address and the rest came from all over the country. The occupations of members were not always given but from the information, certain trends are noticeable. There were many doctors, a fair number of clergymen, and a sprinkling of other professional men. Nevertheless, most were active farmers, active supervisors of their farming tenants, or at least had some vested interest in the land. Those who took a regular part in the activities of the Bath and West (that is, attended meetings, contributed essays, conducted experiments, and competed for premiums) numbered about fifty. Among the Society's warmest supporters and regular attendants at meetings were Dr Charles Parry, Dr Falconer, John Billingsley and Sir Benjamin Hobhouse. There was a very high proportion of passive members who were content to pay their subscriptions and to admire the work from a distance. For example, the 1778 Annual Meeting was attended by only twelve people. After an appeal from the Secretary, attendance rose to thirteen at the next meeting in 1779. After that it hovered around thirty-five for some years. Attendance improved in the 1790s. The annual meeting of 1796 saw a large turnout of 138 which included the Marquis of Lansdowne, the Earls of Stafford, Peterborough and Galloway, and Lord Somerville.

It is quite remarkable how much the Society managed to achieve in its early years on a very small income. The earliest statement of accounts to survive is for the year ending December 1783. It showed total funds in hand to be £477 1s 6d, of which £277 1s 6d were at the bank and the remainder in cash elsewhere. The biggest expense was always the payment of premiums, which absorbed half the annual income. Subscriptions so far received totalled £449 6s 5½d, but many members were in arrears (fig. 5).[25] This was a nagging problem for the Society which persisted well into the new century.

By the beginning of the nineteenth century, the operations of the Society each year included general meetings in the months of February, April, June, September and November, a ploughing match in the summer and, in December, the annual meeting at Hetling House and an exhibition of stock and implements in the Society's yard in James Street West. The December proceedings lasted for three days and included a public dinner. The new century also saw the resignation of William Matthews and the election of Nehemiah Bartley as the new Secretary, by ballot. Bartley was a nurseryman of Lawrence Hill, Bristol.

The Duke of Bedford, who became the President of the Society in 1800, died on 2 March 1802. He was an ardent promoter of agricultural improvement and took an active interest in the Society's affairs, apparently to an extent that was unprecedented among the Society's Presidents. During the general meeting on 22 March, it was decided that a gold medal, equivalent to the value of 20 guineas, should be offered annually as a premium for the greatest improvement in any agriculture-related subject. A premium of 20 guineas was offered for the selected design. A special Bedfordean Committee was appointed for this purpose,

State of the Societies Accounts for the last
Year, and of their Fund this day Dec 18 1783

		£
By Fund in hand at the Settlement made at last Annual Meeting		221.11:2½
Subscriptions brought in at March Meeting		50-8-0
D° at June Meeting		43-1-
D° at Sept. Meeting		23-2-
D° at Dec. Meeting this day		111-4.3
		£449-6:5½

By disbursm^ts b^ot in March Meet^g	70 3-10	
	54 12 11½ }	172-4-11
D° June Meeting	31:2-10	
D° Sept. Meeting	16:5:3½	
D° Dec. Meeting		277-1-6

To Remaining Fund now in hand   277-1-6
Of this Fund there is in Bank   168-1-6 } 277-1-6
In Secretarys hands   109 ---

To which add Subscriptions due for the
present year & Arrears deemed good —   260-0-0

£537-1-6

· Which is 56£ more than the Estimated
Fund was at last Annual Meeting

To deduct for Advertising Bills Rent
& not yet brought in — about   60 —

Total Fund as Estimated this day   £477:1:6

Examined, Sign'd &c = John = Miller

5. The Society's Accounts, 1783. (*Bath Record Office, Bath and West Archives, Vol. 2*) and eventually a design submitted by a Miss Fanshawe was chosen. Mr John Milton of London was commissioned to engrave the die but the committee was unsatisfied with the first impressions taken from it. Matters proceeded slowly, and the committee finally approved the much-corrected die in August 1804. Mr Milton was paid 100 guineas for the die and 20 guineas to cast a gold medal from it (fig. 6).

Obverse   *Reverse*

6. The Bedfordean Medal. (*Letters and Papers, Vol. 10, 1805*)

The first of these gold medals was awarded to Arthur Young for his essay on the nature and properties of manure.[26] The honour of receiving a Bedfordean medal was for several years a much-coveted distinction. It was regarded as the 'blue-ribbon' of the Society and proved a great stimulus to achievement. However, it was later observed that 'considerable latitude seems to have been taken in the bestowal [of the medal]'.[27] For example, it was also awarded to Captain Parry for his Arctic discoveries; to Sir Francis Chantrey, the sculptor, for his bust of Sir Benjamin Hobhouse, President of the Society (1805-1817); and to Mr Clark, the inventor of a life-preserver throwing stick. The connection of these to agriculture is not easily ascertainable.

A recurring theme in the Society's early publications was the application of chemistry to agriculture, especially the chemical analysis of soils and fertilizers. At this time, Lavoisier in Paris was revolutionizing chemistry and applying it to the solution of agricultural problems. It may well have been that his work set English scientists thinking on the same lines. In

1805, a proposal was made by Sir John Coxe Hippisley to establish a
chemical laboratory at the Society's house. This was approved and a
Committee of Chemical Research was set up. The sum of 130 guineas
was raised for establishing and operating a laboratory in the vaults of
Hetling House. Two members stepped forward and generously extended
their assistance: Dr Parry offered to present his chemical apparatus to the
Society, and Dr Clement Archer offered to deliver a course of popular
lectures *gratis* on the principles and application of chemistry to agriculture.
Dr Archer, a Bath physician, also offered his services in superintending
the operation of the laboratory – an offer which was promptly accepted.
Dr Archer was appointed Chemical Professor to the Society and Dr
Cadwallader Boyd his assistant. Farmers were invited to send in samples
of soil for analysis and the results were reported and published by the
Society in its   journals.[28] The following spring, Dr Archer gave a course
of lectures which 'was attended as well by many Ladies and Gentlemen
who had a taste for science, as by most of the Members who remained in
town'.[29] Unfortunately he died a few months later, before completing the
course of lectures. This was finished by his assistant, Dr Boyd, who also
took over the running of the laboratory.

The Society was also very interested in promoting the improvement of
British wool and the establishment of a cloth-mart in Bath. From medieval
times Bath had itself been a clothing town – the ancient monastery had a
shuttle for its coat-of-arms, and special civic privileges were granted to
those who carried on the trade. Although the character of the city changed
when the Hot Springs became fashionable, the old industry, part of that
extending from Frome to Stroud, continued to flourish. Sir Benjamin
Hobhouse was a clothier before he became a banker; Dr Parry wrote and
published frequently on the breed of sheep, and samples of cloth sent by
Lord Somerville and others were discussed at Committee meetings. In
1806, the Secretary reported that he had contracted for a piece of ground
near Kingsmead Square, suitable for an annual exhibition of cattle and
the erection of a cloth-hall. Within six months, this building was finished.
According to Jerom Murch, 'Within my own recollection ... the winter
shows brought a large number of visitors to the city'.[30]

In June 1809, the Prince of Wales became the Patron of the Society and
it was announced that His Royal Highness would pay an annual
subscription of 50 guineas. In December that year the Society approached
the Lords Lieutenant of Somerset, Wiltshire, Gloucester, Hampshire and
Devon, inviting them to become vice-presidents. Apparently what was
good enough for the Prince proved good enough for them and they all

accepted. One would have expected that the Prince's generous subscription would have improved the finances of the Society. However, it was subsequently offered as a premium for growing hemp, a subject about which the Prince felt strongly. The Society obviously did not want to incur the displeasure of the Prince or lose His Royal patronage.

1811 saw the deaths of two of the Society's most active members, Sir John Coxe Hippisley and John Billingsley. Hippisley, as we recall, had proposed the institution of a chemical laboratory at the Society's rooms, and his services to the Society were suitably acknowledged. However, Billingsley was given a hero's treatment and a portrait of him was placed in a conspicuous part of the Society's Great Room, with the following inscription:

JOHN BILLINGSLEY, Esq.

One of the original Founders, one of the greater Ornaments, and for 32 Years, a most able and active VICE-PRESIDENT, of this INSTITUTION, whose Ardour in acquiring Knowledge was only equalled by his Delight in imparting it; and whose Zeal in promoting Objects of public Utility was as conspicuous as his Judgment in discerning, and his Ability in carrying them into Effect.

The BATH and WEST of ENGLAND SOCIETY

In grateful Remembrance of his transcendent Merits, have caused this Tablet to be inscribed.

Meanwhile, the problem of members in arrears persisted and became so serious that in 1813 the Secretary, Robert Ricards, was driven to printing a black list of the defaulters in the hope of shaming them into payment. In 1818 the Secretary gave notice of his intention to resign due to his failing health. Benjamin Leigh Lye, a former Army Captain, was elected to that office.

Between the 1820s and the 1840s, the Society slipped into a period of decline. By this time the original impetus of the Society had faded and signs of decay began to manifest themselves. It had lost some of its most able members and was beset by financial problems.The existing members also began to lose interest in the activities of the Society for several reasons. Firstly, the improvements made in agriculture in the last few decades were so great that many entertained the idea that the objectives of the

Society had been accomplished. Secondly, as a result of the agricultural depression due to the Napoleonic Wars, the farming community was very unpopular and held responsible for the scarcity and costliness of food. Therefore, they were the last persons to be supported. Lastly, there was the competition of other societies, such as those at Bruton and Frome. For example, in 1849 one of the Society's vice-presidents, Sir Alex Hood, Bart, resigned, explaining that he had 'so much occupation in attending agricultural meetings in the western division that he cannot attend at Bath also'.[31] Under such adverse forces, the Society's finances suffered a severe blow. In 1820, the income from subscriptions had fallen from £591 in the previous year to £288. In 1821, the Secretary, Leigh Lye, voluntarily took a 50% pay cut. In 1822, the Committee of Superintendence reported:

> While this meeting did realize with regret that there has been a considerable reduction in the receipts of the Society, it did not fail also to notice that the expences have been so diminished as to leave but a small balance against the Society. It is hoped that by care and attention in offering and lessening Premiums and by the strictest economy in managing the affairs of the Society the disbursements will be kept at the lowest possible point and that it may surely be left to the zeal, spirit and perseverance of the members and friends of the Institution to prevent its receipts from suffering a further decrease.[32]

The gold Bedfordean Medal became a silver medal due to the faltering finances of the Society. After two or three interregnums, it disappeared altogether from the Society's premiums around the early 1830s. The premium list itself was thoroughly revised and severely limited. Furthermore, the loss of some of the Society's leading members added to its misfortunes. In 1829, Volume 15 of *Letters and Papers* was published.[33] This was thirteen years after the publication of Volume 14 and the Society commented:

> In the interval which is specified, the Society has been deprived of many of its most distinguished Members, [and the] loss of so much energy and talent would naturally paralize, to a certain extent, the proceedings of the remaining body.

Between 1833 and 1840, there were four resignations and eight deaths in the ranks of the vice-presidents. Furthermore, members lacked the enthusiasm and efficiency of those of the earlier period and interest in the Society's activities was continually decreasing. For example, in 1834 one member withdrew his subscription, stating that the Society was not conducted as it used to be. Nevertheless, the Society continued to conduct its business as normally and as best it could. In 1836, the Committee of Superintendence reported a larger than usual turnout at the annual ploughing match, and came to the conclusion that this 'may be taken as a gratifying evidence, that, notwithstanding the numerous Agricultural Societies which are every where springing up around us, the leading objects of this most ancient Society are not becoming less useful or less attractive'.[34]

The situation did not improve, and in 1840 the Society was forced to sell £300 of its investments. The bad fortune continued when its bankers, Hobhouse, Phillott and Lowder, proprietors of the old Bath Bank in Milsom Street, failed, owing the Society £411 2s 9d. In the event, the Society managed to retrieve about £267 in dividends, which amounted to the loss of about a year's income. Tugwell, Mackenzie and Clutterbuck were appointed as the new bankers, but the main problem seemed to be finding the money to pay into this new account.

In 1847, the Secretary was directed to give the landlord notice unless a reduction in rent was made because the Society felt that the rent for their rooms at Hetling House was too high. The rent was subsequently reduced from £40 to £30 per annum. However, by December 1848, in view of diminishing income, the Society gave up their rooms. The reason they gave was that the reduced rent was still too high and the premises were 'in such a bad state of repair as to render the occupation at times extremely inconvenient'.[35] As a result the books and various articles belonging to the Society were moved from Hetling House and placed under the care of the Bath Commercial and Literary Institution, without any payment for rent.[36] By arrangement with the latter organization, the Society's annual meetings were also held at their rooms without charge.

In 1849, Leigh Lye, the Secretary, was too ill to carry on his duties and handed in his resignation. His 'regularity and ability in all matters relating to the business of the Society' was acknowledged. His successor was Henry St John Maule, and it was recognized that 'having a regard to the pecuniary circumstances of the Society, the office should be an honorary one'.[37] In general, the 1840s were marked by the Society's attempts to economize further, and to find ways of increasing its funds. They were largely unsuccessful and in 1850 the Society's cash in hand amounted to a mere £310 5s 6d.[38]

Despite the gloomy outlook in the 1820s, 1830s and 1840s, the few who soldiered on did so in the hope that in the Society's middle age, 'the members

who are already enrolled in its list will exert themselves to maintain its
ancient prosperity and their own celebrity, and that, by a new accession
of strength, the Bath and West of England may spring up, like a giant
refreshed, and preserve the vigour and usefulness which have distinguished
the earlier periods of its existence'.[39] Fortunately, their efforts paid off and
the Society was given a new lease of life by the enthusiasm and resource-
fulness of a few members like Sir Thomas Dyke Acland and William Miles,
MP. Acland of Killerton was a west country squire who retired from
Parliament in 1847 in order to devote himself to the management of his
estates. In 1850, he presented to the Society a scheme for its reorganization.
He suggested that it should move its annual meeting away from Bath
and hold it each year in a different town within the Society's area,
combined with a show of machinery and livestock. He cited the Royal
Agricultural Society show at Exeter in 1850 as a fine example, and was
determined to bring all the advantages of such an exhibition within the
reach of the western counties. Acland's proposal was strongly supported
by Miles and the Society's President, Lord Portman. Meetings were held
in Bath, Bridgwater, Taunton, Exeter and elsewhere to ascertain the
willingness of gentlemen holding land in the western counties to support
the scheme for meeting in different parts of the region. The response was
positive. In addition, a negotiation was opened between the Bath and
West and the Devon Agricultural Society with a view to uniting the two.
The result was a merger on 11 February 1851 and a new constitution.

The first annual meeting and show under the new constitution was held
in Taunton in 1852. It generated a lot of local and national interest and support
and stockbreeders and trade exhibitors came from all over the country.
This set the Society on the road to recovery. By the end of the 1850s, the
regenerated Society began to feel reasonably secure when it became
apparent that its new policies were working successfully. As a sign of its
renewed vitality, a second series of journals was launched in 1853 under
the editorship of Acland. The Society was set to face the world once more.

Conclusion

The Society had come about at a time when the western counties needed
it most. As set out in 1777, the Society's aim was to 'excite by premiums a
spirit of emulation and improvement in such parts of husbandry as seem
most to require it'.[40] At the time of the Society's inception, farming in the
western counties was in a backward state. The farmer was guided in his

work by custom, or such modifications as observation and experience might permit. Crops were small and the quantity of grain inferior. The implements employed were very limited in number and simple in construction.

In assessing the extent of the Society's success, one can safely say that it had gone a long way towards fulfilling the objectives of the founder-members. It had spent a great deal of money on premiums to encourage experiment, innovation and invention. It had built up an extensive correspondence with agriculturalists both at home and abroad. It had published the kind of articles and letters which it believed would help to raise the general level of efficiency in the west country. It had collected useful information, drawings and models from all parts of the country. It had put on an annual show that attracted both exhibitors and visitors from all over the country.

In analyzing the operations of the Bath and West, one is struck by the diversity of subjects to which it had directed its attention and, at times, its success.[41] It was instrumental in the introduction of improved turnip-husbandry into the western counties. Great pains were also taken to introduce new seeds, and much attention given to new varieties of vegetables. It must be recognized that the Society was essentially operating at a time when England was shut out from the Continent, and the necessity of fostering home industries of every description was a matter of vital importance. Further, the fact that it attempted to stimulate improvement and invention by the novelty of the premium system must not go unrecognized.[42]

The Society's early history is inextricably bound up with the history of the city of Bath. For seventy-four years from 1777-1851, the Society held its meetings in Bath; its business was carried out at Hetling House; livestock was exhibited in the yard at Walcot; and its leading members were drawn from the city. After 1851, the close links with the city grew weaker when the Society decided to hold its annual meeting and show at different towns in the western region.[43] It returned to Bath for its annual show in 1854, and once more in 1877, rather significantly, for its centenary show. Nevertheless during this time the Society retained a Bath address, first at 16 Pulteney Street, in the residence of its Secretary, Henry St John Maule, and later at 4 Terrace Walk towards the end of the century. In 1905 it established itself at 3 Pierrepont Street where it remained until 1974. In 1964, after many years of holding peripatetic shows around the region, it acquired a 212-acre area of grass farmland near Shepton Mallet, Somerset. Since 1965, the Society's show and activities have been held on this permanent site. But to this day, the Society retains its Bath connections. Its archives are housed at the city's Record Office and its collection of printed books is in the care of the University of Bath.

Appendix 1

AIMS OF THE SOCIETY, 1777 [44]

The principal object of this society's attention will be,

To excite by premiums a spirit of emulation and improvement in such parts of husbandry as seem most to require it:

To endeavour to increase the annual produce of corn, by bringing into cultivation, in the least expensive and most effectual manner, such lands as are at present barren or badly cultivated, particularly by draining and manuring; and by the introduction of various sorts of vegetable food for cattle:

To promote the knowledge of agriculture by encouraging and directing regular experiments on those subjects which are of the most importance to it, by distributing rewards to such persons as shall raise the largest and best crops both of natural and artificial grasses, and the several species of grain, on any given quantity of ground:

To encourage planting on waste lands, raising of quick hedges, cultivating turnips, Scotch cabbages, &c, &c:

To promote all improvements in the various implements belonging to the farmer, and introducing such *new* ones as the experience of other counties has proved more valuable than those generally in use:

This society's attention will also be directed to all improvements of the machines used in our different manufactories, as well as the manufactures themselves; and to encourage ingenuity, diligence, and honesty, in servants and labourers:

And to sum up the whole, everything that is conducive to the prosperity of the counties of Somerset, Wilts, Gloucester, and Dorset, and the good of the community at large, will be diligently attended by this society.

Appendix 2

SECRETARIES & PRESIDENTS OF THE SOCIETY, 1777-1852

Secretaries		*Presidents*	
1777-1787	Edmund Rack	1777-1780	Earl of Ilchester
1787-1800	William Matthews	1780-1798	Marquis of Ailesbury
1800-1805	Nehemiah Bartley	1798-1800	Lord Somerville
1805-1818	Robert Ricards	1800-1802	1st Duke of Bedford
1818-1849	Benjamin Leigh Lye	1802-1805	2nd Duke of Bedford
1849-1865	Henry St John Maule	1805-1817	Sir Benjamin Hobhouse
		1817-1847	Marquis of Lansdowne
		1847-1852	Lord Portman

Notes

1   D.G.C. Allan, *William Shipley: Founder of the Royal Society of Arts* (1979),p.12.
2   For the agricultural activities of the Royal Society, see R.V. Lennard, 'English Agriculture under Charles II', *Economic History Review*, Vol. 3 (1932), pp.23-45.
3   H. Edmund, 'History of the Brecknockshire Agricultural Society, 1755-1955', *Brycheiniog*, Vol. 2 (1956), pp.22-65.
4   The use of the premium system was not restricted to agriculture alone. At the time, it was also used to stimulate invention in industry, manufactures and engineering.
5   It appears that Rack, who was asthmatic and had suffered a serious bout of jaundice, became one of the earliest dupes of the notorious quack, Dr Graham, who was patronized by Mrs Macaulay.
6   W. Lewis, *A Century of Agricultural Progress* (Bath, 1879),pp.29-30.
7   *Ibid.*, p.30.
8   Bath Record Office (BRO), Bath and West Archives, Vol. 2, 8 September 1777.
9   Fellowship of the Royal Society was for life and represented the highest attainment in British science.
10   G. Winters, *A New and Compendious System of Husbandry* (Bristol, 1787), p.12.
11   *Rules and Orders of the Society, instituted at Bath, for the encouragement of agriculture, arts, manufactures, commerce, mechanics and the fine arts* (Bath, 1777).
12   BRO, Bath and West Archives, Vol. 2, 13 November 1777.
13   At this time, Priestley was Librarian to the Earl of Shelburne at Bowood.
14   Both Davy and Arawen were elected at the Annual Meeting of 1804. BRO, Bath and West Archives, Vol. 7, 11 December 1804.
15   E. Rack, *Essays, Letters and Poems* (Bath, 1781).
16   BRO, Bath and West Archives, Vol. 2, 13 November 1777.

17 BRO, Bath and West Archives, Vol. 2, 13 December 1777.
18 The Royal Society had tried to use this method to collect similar information in the 1660s. They received only eleven reports. The Bath Society was more successful and the results were published in their journal, *Letters and Papers*, Vol.1 (1780).
19 BRO, Bath and West Archives, Vol. 2, 14 December 1779.
20 Sometimes spelt 'Bethell' or 'Bethel'.
21 *Letters and Papers*, Vol. 1 (1780), p.5.
22 BRO, Bath and West Archives, Vol. 2, 14 November 1786, 12 December 1786.
23 Hetling House appears to have been built c.1570 by Edward Clarke on Norman foundations and leased soon afterwards to Sir Walter Hungerford of Farleigh (d.1585). It is believed that the poet Alexander Pope lived there. It subsequently became Abbey Church House and was restored in the 1950s after air-raid damage during World War II. Bath Public Library, E7/298; K. Hudson, *The Bath and West: A Bicentenary History* (Bradford-on-Avon, 1976), p.236, fn.5.
24 BRO, Bath and West Archives, Vol. 2, 8 April 1788.
25 BRO, Bath and West Archives, Vol. 2, page facing 8 December 1783.
26 200 copies of this essay were printed for distribution in pamphlet form and subsequently reprinted in *Letters and Papers*, Vol. 9 (1802), pp.97-198.
27 Lewis, *op. cit.*, p.45.
28 The first of these results were published in *Letter and Papers*, Vol. 11(1807), pp.275-313. According to Russell, these were the earliest of its kind that he had seen. E.J. Russell, *A History of Agricultural Science in Great Britain* (1966).
29 W.J. Williams and D.M. Stoddart, *Bath – Some Encounters with Science* (Bath, 1978).
30 J. Murch, 'The History and Literature of the Bath and West of England and Southern Counties Society', *Journal of the Bath and West of England Society* (1890-1), pp.144-5.
31 *Rules and Orders*, 'Report of the Committee of Superintendence' (1849), p.19. Robert Blagdon Hale, MP, Vice-President, also resigned in the same year, giving the same reason as Hood.
32 BRO, Bath and West Archives, Vol. 8, 7 December 1822.
33 This was to be the last volume of *Letters and Papers*.
34 *Rules and Orders*, 'Report of the Committee of Superintendence' (1836), p.47.
35 *Rules and Orders*, 'Report of the Committee of Superintendence' (1849), p.19.
36 The Bath Commercial and Literary Institution (BCLI) must not be confused with the Bath Literary and Scientific Institution (BLSI). They were two separate organizations. The Bath and West had first approached the BLSI about this matter. However, the BLSI would only retain the Bath and West's possessions if an annual rent was charged. This caused the latter to look elsewhere in the hope of finding an institution of 'more kindred public character' that would not make a charge. At this point they were approached by the BCLI. *Rules and Orders*, 'Report of the Committee of Superintendence' (1851), p.19.
37 *Ibid.*, p.20.
38 *Rules and Orders*, (1851), p.16.
39 *Rules and Orders*, 'Report of the Committee of Superintendence' (1839), p.42.
40 *Rules and Orders*, (1777), p.vii.

41   The Society's journals provide an invaluable source of information on the startlingly wide range of activities carried on within the Society. It concerned itself with issues from descriptions of ploughs and mills to the utility of Friendly Societies and Rev Malthus's population theory. Some may appear trivial, but show the liberal stance adopted by the Society.
42   It has been written that the Society 'preferred taking a hopeful view of every suggested improvement and new invention rather than that genius should be neglected or merit go unrewarded'. Lewis, *op.cit.*, p.84.
43   The 'nomad' existence of the Society in those years may help to explain the lack of documents to have survived from this period. It was not uncommon for the Society to hold its meetings at hotels in whichever town it happened to be holding its show that year.
44   *Rules and Orders*, (1777), pp.v-vii.

Acknowledgements

I would like to extend my appreciation to the Royal Bath and West of England Society who have permitted me to consult their archives and library, and the Society's Honorary Archivist, Colin Johnston, for his assistance with the materials.

ARTISTS' PICTURE ROOMS IN EIGHTEENTH-CENTURY BATH

Susan Legouix Sloman

In May 1775 David Garrick described to Hannah More the sense of well-being he experienced in Bath: 'I do this, & do that, & do Nothing, & I go here and go there and go nowhere – Such is ye life of Bath & such the Effects of this place upon me – I forget my Cares, & my large family in London, & Every thing ...'.[1] The visitor to Bath in the second half of the eighteenth century had very few decisions to make once he was safely installed in his lodgings. A well-established pattern of bathing, drinking spa water, worship, concert and theatre-going and balls meant that in the early and later parts of each day he was likely to be fully occupied. However he was free to decide how to spend the daylight hours between around 10am when the company generally left the Pump Room and 3pm when most people retired to their lodgings to dine. Contemporary diaries and journals suggest that favourite daytime pursuits included walking on the parades, carriage excursions, visiting libraries (which were usually also bookshops), milliners, toy shops, jewellers and artists' showrooms and of course, sitting for a portrait.

At least 160 artists spent some time working in Bath in the eighteenth century,[2] a statistic which indicates that sitting for a portrait was indeed one of the most popular activities. Although he did not specifically have Bath in mind, Thomas Bardwell noted in 1756, 'It is well known, that no Nation in the World delights so much in Face-painting, or gives so generous Encouragement to it as our own'.[3] In 1760 the Bath writer Daniel Webb noted 'the extraordinary passion which the English have for portraits'.[4] André Rouquet in his survey of *The Present State of the Arts in England* of 1755 described how 'Every portrait painter in England has a room to shew his pictures, separate from that in which he works. People who have nothing to do, make it one of their morning amusements to go and see these collections'.[5] Since there were by the mid eighteenth century plenty of visitors in Bath with 'nothing to do', it follows that artists would have done their best to attract people to their rooms and hoped to win new patrons from among the idle viewers. In fact in Bath the display of an artist's work was probably his most important form of advertising. Not every painter could afford the luxury of a room permanently set aside for exhibition as well as a room in which to paint, although the most eminent artists such as William Hoare (1707-92), Thomas Gainsborough (1727-88), Robert Edge Pine (c.1730-88), Thomas Beach (1738-1806) and Joseph Wright (1734-97) certainly did[6] (fig. 1).

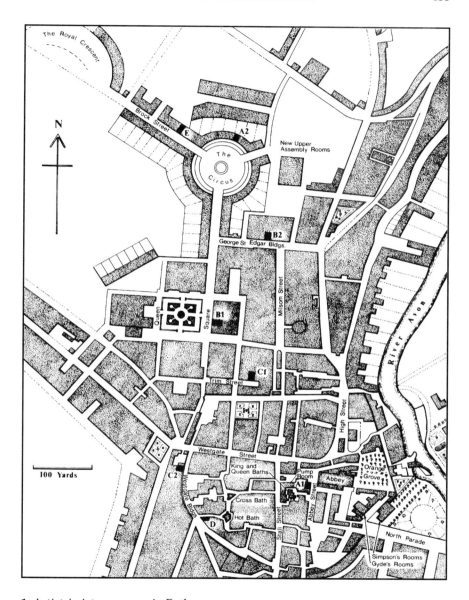

1. Artists' picture rooms in Bath:
A1, A2 – Thomas Gainsborough; B1, B2 – William Hoare; C1, C2 – Thomas Beach;
D – Robert Edge Pine; E – Joseph Wright.

Hoare was in Bath from 1738 until his death, with only a few periods of absence; Gainsborough from October 1758 until spring 1759 and then from late autumn 1759 until autumn 1774; Pine from 1772-79; Beach on and off from 1772-1803; and Wright of Derby from November 1775 until June 1777.

Of the 160 or so recorded painters, at least half were miniaturists, who seem to have rented or begged display space in a variety of commercial premises in the town. Andrew Rymsdyk (1753/4-86), for example, advised prospective customers at the beginning of the autumn 1786 season that specimens of his work could be seen 'Every day at Mr Meyler's Circulating Library in the Grove, where Ladies and Gentlemen will please to leave their address'. He described his work as 'Portraits drawn in small ... and put into the most fashionable frame that ever was invented'.[7] Peter Ogier (fl.1793-1800), miniaturist, showed his work at Lintern's Music Shop in Abbey Churchyard, while Francis Laine (1721-1810), another miniaturist, showed at the shop belonging to Mr Butt, peruke-maker in Orange Grove.[8] Thomas Worlidge (1700-66) sold his portraits and prints through Mrs Wicksteed's well-known toy shop in Orange Grove, and successfully combined business and family life by making the Wicksteeds' daughter his third wife when he was sixty-three years old.[9]

Miniatures which needed almost no drying time and could easily be fitted into ready-made frames were particularly suited to the transitory Bath clientele, but at the same time a healthy demand existed for oil portraits, reaching a peak between 1760 and 1780. The most successful painters of oil portraits probably all had separate picture display rooms and painting rooms as described by Rouquet, and some had more than one display room. One of the reasons that separate exhibition rooms were so essential was that painting time and viewing hours coincided, both taking advantage of the brightest daylight of the Bath winter season. While visitors were occasionally admitted to watch artists at work, most painters probably preferred to work undisturbed and to rely on a footman or assistant to welcome visitors and deal with enquiries. Only the young Thomas Lawrence (1769-1830), who was promoted by his father as a child prodigy, seems to have willingly worked in front of an audience. (One Bath visitor who watched Lawrence at work was as captivated by the beauty of his luxuriant, wavy hair as by his artistic ability.[10]) In contemporary records, viewing rooms are called picture rooms or show rooms, often spelt 'shew' rooms. In 1763 Gainsborough described his as his 'best parlour to show Pictures in'.[11] The room in which the artist worked was invariably referred to as the 'painting room', the Italian word *studio* not coming into general usage in England until the nineteenth century.

Diarists and letter writers John Baker, Mary Delany, Mary Hamilton, Samuel Ireland, Elizabeth Noel, Eliza Orlebar, John Penrose and Dorothy Richardson all record visiting Gainsborough's Bath picture rooms (see Appendix below), but their accounts are all disappointingly bland. Much more evocative is a letter written by Horace Walpole on 9 June 1781 in which he described in some detail an enjoyable morning spent at Thomas Beach's house at 2 Westgate Buildings, Bath. Beach had been a pupil of Reynolds in London and though hardly an exciting or innovative artist, had an acknowledged gift for capturing a likeness (fig. 2). Walpole attended

> a little private concert, in the picture rooms of Mr Beach of Bath. Amongst the performers were the celebrated Mr Salomon, Sig. Tenducci, and Miss Guest ... A fine light and shade being thrown upon the paintings, every one found himself surrounded, as if by magic, by a number of his acquaintances, breathing in canvass ... About fifty ladies and gentlemen formed the audience; and, in such natural shapes did the pictures look upon, and seem to listen to us, that it was difficult to persuade ourselves they were not auditors also.[12]

It is little wonder Walpole was impressed by this entertainment. The German violinist, Johann Peter Salomon, had made his first British appearance at Covent Garden only three months before and was in Bath to lead a concert for the benefit of the Pauper Charity on 31 May 1781.[13] Giusto Ferdinando Tenducci, the Italian castrato, was a colourful character who had long been popular in Bath. Miss Mary Jane Guest was the most talented keyboard performer in Bath, at this time at the threshold of a successful career as a performer and teacher. This high-quality musical gathering must have been a powerful bait to attract visitors to Beach's rooms. From Walpole's description it seems the portraits were carefully lit, perhaps artificially, even though the concert was in the morning.[14] Unfortunately this appears to be the only account of a concert in a picture room in Bath: one can only speculate as to whether this was a unique occasion or whether it followed precedents staged by Gainsborough or Hoare, both of whom were keenly musical.

A year after the Beach concert, in November 1782, a Mr Bateman presented Philippe De Loutherbourg's *Eidophusikon* in rooms on the opposite side of Westgate Buildings which had formerly been Robert Edge Pine's picture rooms. The *Eidophusikon* was a display of panoramic pictures animated by moving lights in order to suggest effects of weather, fire, the sun and moon and other natural phenomena. Visitors to this

2. Miss Julia Keasberry by Thomas Beach (1738-1806), 1782. Oil on canvas, 158.0 x 140.0cm. (*Photograph by courtesy of Sotheby's, London*)

exhibition could also enjoy further transparent paintings by De Loutherbourg, stained glass by Thomas Jervais, and copies by John Powell of Sir Joshua Reynolds' *Nativity* and *Marlborough Family*.[15] Whereas at the London performances of the *Eidophusikon* Michael Arne had played on the harpsichord, in Bath Joseph Wilkins played Handel 'and other distinguished masters' on the organ.[16] De Loutherbourg was also a designer for the stage and the *Eidophusikon* was in itself a piece of theatre without actors.

Thomas Beach's attempt to add sound and drama to the portrait painter's picture display room is just one instance of the way in which the arts of painting, music and theatre interrelated and nurtured one another at this period. A sale of Thomas Beach's studio effects in Bath in 1803 included portraits of Tenducci and actors John Henderson and Mrs Siddons,[17] and it does appear that artists deliberately retained portraits of performers and other well-known characters as show-piece works to hang in their picture rooms, and painted versions of commissioned portraits expressly for this purpose. The intention was clearly to present to the picture room visitors the faces of individuals they had recently seen at the theatre or assembly rooms, so that they could judge for themselves how good a likeness the artist achieved. Portraits of David Garrick proliferated at this time and many were probably used for this purpose. A portrait of Garrick hung in Robert Edge Pine's picture room in Bath[18] and a Mrs Collins, profile and miniature painter, advertised a portrait of Garrick at her premises at 6 Bond Street, Bath in the *Bath Chronicle* of 11 February 1779.[19] In a letter to David Garrick written from Bath, Gainsborough explained that one reason for the delay in delivering his portrait was that he wanted to make a copy of it to hang in his own parlour, 'not as a show Picture, but for my own enjoyment'.[20] The fact that Gainsborough stated that this copy was *not* a 'show Picture' suggests that it was normal practice to paint show pictures.

A documented show picture which relates specifically to Bath is a double portrait by Joseph Wright of Derby (fig. 3). Wright settled in Bath in November 1775, possibly on the recommendation of the former Bath resident artist Ozias Humphry whose company he had enjoyed in Italy in June and July of the same year.[21] Wright occupied a house on the north side of Brock Street, just off the Circus, probably the one now numbered 29.[22] Unlike Gainsborough in the late 1750s, Wright was not overwhelmed with commissions on his arrival and in April 1776 he confided to his brother, 'I am now painting a half-length of Dr. Wilson and his adopted daughter Miss Macauley (*sic*); this is for reputation only, but you must not say so'.[23]

3. *The Rev Thomas Wilson D.D. with his adopted daughter Miss Macaulay* by Joseph Wright (1734-97), 1776. Oil on canvas, 101.5 x 127.0cm. (*Photograph by courtesy of Sotheby's, London*)

Dr Thomas Wilson, son of the Bishop of Sodor and Man, was Rector of St Stephen's, Walbrook in London, but kept a Bath residence, Alfred House in Alfred Street and was a familiar figure in Bath society with a face that would have been instantly recognizable to picture room visitors. For a short time Wilson idolized the authoress and historian Mrs Catherine Macaulay, showering her with gifts and favours in a manner which he lived to regret. He celebrated her birthday in April 1777 with an extraordinarily lavish entertainment at Alfred House.[24] The double portrait of Wilson and Mrs Macaulay's young daughter which Wright painted in an attempt to promote his portrait practice may have been purchased by Wilson or given to him on Wright's return to Derby in 1777. It must have still been in Bath in 1781 when the twelve-year old Thomas Lawrence copied the figure of Wilson (carefully omitting Miss Macaulay) for an engraving to be given to subscribers to Cruttwell's *The Works of ... Thomas Wilson ... Bishop of Sodor and Man*.[25] By September 1782 and probably earlier, Lawrence was living just a few doors along from Wilson's house, at 2 Alfred Street. Even though Joseph Wright's show-piece portrait failed to bring in commissions, it must have had an effect on the young Lawrence and may also have inspired William Hoare's attractive double portrait of the poet *Christopher Anstey with his daughter Mary*, painted around 1779 and now in the National Portrait Gallery.

Mrs Macaulay herself was painted in Bath by Robert Edge Pine who settled in the city in 1772 (fig. 4). The Pine family's association with Bath has its roots much earlier in the century, when Robert's father John Pine engraved the thirteen plates for the architect John Wood's *Essay towards a Description of Bath*, published in Bath in 1742. It is known from Bateman's advertisements for the *Eidophusikon* that Robert Edge Pine's rooms at Hetling Court off Westgate Buildings were grand and spacious. One of the press notices announces, 'Mr Bateman has engaged for the purpose of these exhibitions, the House in Westgate-Buildings lately occupied by Mr Pine, which contains a suit (*sic*) of apartments happily calculated to display the whole series of effects to the utmost advantage'.[26] In another advertisement Bateman added 'The door next the Hot Bath Pump Room in Hetling Court will be open for the admission of company in the morning. Care will be taken to keep the several rooms constantly well aired'.[27] It is evident that Pine's house was adjacent to the Hot Bath Pump Room, a perfect site from which to attract visitors. Westgate Buildings was also on the direct carriage route from the Circus, a factor which must have influenced both Beach and Pine in their choice of rooms. By the 1770s the Circus was the hub of Bath's social life, being one of the prime new residential locations with the New or Upper Assembly Rooms just a matter of yards away.

4. *Mrs Catherine Macaulay*, attributed to Robert Edge Pine (c.1730-1788), c.1777. Oil on canvas, 73.4 x 62.2cm. (*Photograph by courtesy of the National Portrait Gallery*)

At the end of 1766 Gainsborough had moved with the tide uphill to the Circus, but during the first half of his stay in Bath he had taken a house situated, like Pine's, right next to one of the principal bathing establishments. The ground floor of Gainsborough's first town house in

5. Model of Gainsborough's house, Abbey Street, Bath. The house was demolished following the discovery of the Roman Baths in 1892. Gainsborough leased the house from 1760-1774 and worked here from 1760-1766.

Abbey Street actually incorporated a public passageway to the King's and Queen's Baths (fig. 5). This house, which Gainsborough called his 'House in the smoake',[28] was brand new when the artist became the first tenant in May 1760. It stood very near the south-west corner of Bath Abbey, making the corner of Abbey Churchyard and Abbey Street, with its front door opening on to Abbey Street.[29] The room in which Gainsborough displayed his paintings was the 'best parlour', the principal ground floor room to the left of the front door. The other large room on the ground floor to the right of the front door was home to a millinery run by Gainsborough's sister Mary Gibbon. In common with other milliners in Bath at this time Mrs Gibbon would have sold dress fabrics, lace, flowers and perfumes, as well as hats. Exotic perfumes must have wafted through from Mrs Gibbon's shop to the picture room and in many respects her

6. *Harriet, Viscountess Tracy* by Thomas Gainsborough (1727-1788), c.1763. Oil on canvas, 126.4 x 101.0cm. (*Photograph by courtesy of Gainsborough's House, Sudbury*)

business must have complemented her brother's portrait practice. Her merchandise may well be represented in some of the female portraits which hung in the best parlour. Between 1762 and 1766 Gainsborough produced a notable series of Van Dyck-inspired three-quarter length female portraits in which rich fabric, lace and flowers feature prominently. *Mary, Lady Carr*, at the Yale Center for British Art, New Haven, and *Harriet, Viscountess Tracy*, at Gainsborough's House, Sudbury (fig. 6), are particularly dazzling examples. When Gainsborough arrived in Bath he had searched for a property where 'a good painting room as to light, a proper access etc., could be had'.[30] The light was clearly important for painting, and the access for visitors to the picture room and for sitters. The public access at Abbey Street could scarcely have been improved upon. Abbey Street was a busy pedestrian and sedan chair route leading from the Pump Room and Bath Abbey to the two Lower Assembly Rooms (the Upper Rooms were not to open until 1771), the theatre and the Parades. Most visitors to Bath in the early 1760s would have unavoidably passed his door more than once a day. A depiction of the house by Thomas Malton of 1784 shows a flat, almost certainly wooden, sign board just above the ground floor windows (fig. 7). It reads BATH BANK, signifying the business which subsequently occupied Gainsborough's picture room. It is quite likely that a similar board advertised the painter's presence some years earlier: Philip Thicknesse deplored the fact that even the most eminent painters in Bath placed name boards on their houses, a practice which he considered both vulgar and inappropriate.[31] Slightly earlier artists, in common with other traders, used hanging signs with pictures or symbols rather than name boards, it being assumed that those with money to spend were not necessarily literate. In London Hogarth had a hanging sign with Van Dyck's head and a minor artist, S. Morley, a Golden Head, while in Bath as late as 1762 Thomas Worlidge marked his house in Stall Street with a Golden Head.[32] In Bath in the 1740s, engraver Jacob Skinner wittily advertised the sign of a Grasshopper, a play on this own name, since grasshoppers shed their skins.[33]

Although Gainsborough may well have used a name board in Abbey Street, the splendour of his house must have acted as an advertisement in itself. In an awkwardly restricted site John Wood had designed a classic town house which seems to have been intended as a Bath residence for Evelyn, 2nd Duke of Kingston. The pediment was boldly carved with the Duke's crest, enriching the façade and distinguishing the house from its neighbours.[34] It was one of the most expensive houses in Bath, costing £150 a year in rent in the 1760s, more for exmple than 1 Royal Crescent whose tenants, including the Duke and Duchess of York, paid £140.[35] For Gainsborough the investment in a grand property paid off: commissions

7. *North East View of the Abbey Church at Bath* (mistakenly entitled: it should read *South East View ...*) (*detail*) **by James Gandon after Thomas Malton (1748-1804),** **1784. Aquatint, whole image size 33.0 x 48.0cm.** The house seen in shadow to the left is Gainsborough's. (*Photograph courtesy of the Victoria Art Gallery, Bath & North East Somerset Council*)

flooded in, 'he could live in the style of a gentleman, and entertain company'[36] and his establishment was nicknamed 'Gain's borough'.[37] In London in the following decade the portraitist Tilly Kettle employed the same tactics but with less talent and unhappier results. According to Edward Edwards, 'Thinking he might acquire more notice by an increase of shew, [Kettle] built for himself a house in Old Bond-street, opposite Burlington-gardens, soon after which he became bankrupt ...'.[38] Thomas Lawrence, who was introduced to portrait painting in Bath, was always conscious of the need for a prestigious address and when he moved to London, struggled to pay for his ambitious lifestyle. Thomas Barker, who also learnt his trade in Bath and was profoundly influenced by Gainsborough, took Benjamin Vandergucht's large exhibition room in Lower Brook Street, London after the latter's death in 1794.[39]

At Abbey Street, Gainsborough's picture room measured 24ft by 20ft 8ins, a sizeable space, but probably smaller than Francis Cotes's 'shew room' in London.[40] The exact size of Cotes's room is unknown, but on the floor he had an Indian carpet measuring 22ft 6ins by 14ft 6ins and a Turkey carpet of 9ft by 7ft 7ins, suggesting a very generously-proportioned space. Thomas Beach's picture room in Bath, as has already been shown, could accommodate a seated audience of fifty and a group of musicians. Gainsborough's Abbey Street show room was undoubtedly well suited to showing the increasingly large canvases he produced between 1760 and 1766. The rooms at 17 Circus, where the artist lived and worked from 1767 until 1774, were slightly smaller, and it is a fact that Gainsborough did not paint anything as large as *General Honeywood* (Ringling Museum, Sarasota, Florida) or *The Byam Family* (Marlborough College, Marlborough) after his move to the upper town.

At the Circus, Gainsborough's principal picture room was probably the main south-facing room on the first floor, adjoining the painting room, from which it would have been separated by double doors.[41] In a letter written in 1773 from the Circus to his friend and sitter, the well-known preacher Dr William Dodd, Gainsborough described how he secretly watched observers reacting to Dodd's portrait. It appears from this particularly animated and amusing account that the artist could not resist eavesdropping on his picture room visitors from the painting room. He tells Dodd that he had considered further improvements to the portrait, but 'the ladies say it is very handsome as it is; for I peep & listen through the keyhole of the door of the painting room on purpose to see how you touch them out of the pulpit as well as in it. Lord! says one, what a lively eye that gentleman has!'[42] An early nineteenth-century watercolour by

8. *A Portrait Painter's Ante-Room* by Thomas Rowlandson (1756-1827), 1809. Pencil, pen and ink and watercolour, 12.4 x 20.1cm. (*Photograph by courtesy of the Ashmolean Museum, Oxford*)

Thomas Rowlandson shows an arrangement of artist's rooms which is probably very like that found by visitors to Gainsborough's house at the Circus (fig. 8). A show room is buzzing with chattering visitors while an obsequious footman opens a door for a sitter to enter an adjoining painting room where the artist waits. The huge number of paintings seen on the wall in Rowlandson's drawing serves as a reminder that the picture display room must have housed drying-out commissioned portraits as well as show pictures. An average period of about five months elapsed between initial portrait sittings and delivery of the finished work[43] and as can be deduced from Gainsborough's letter to Dodd, the normal procedure must have been to hang up completed paintings until they were dry enough to be varnished.

In London, Francis Cotes's painting room and show room adjoined, and both were furnished with rich carpets and mahogany furniture. Sir Joshua Reynolds had a London house to which he 'added a splendid gallery for the exhibition of his paintings and a commodious and elegant room for his sitters', while George Romney had 'a painting room with perfect light, and a capacious show room well fitted for the artist'.[44] It is to be expected that artists in Bath would have offered similar stylish furnishings and home comforts. When 2 Westgate Buildings was advertised in January and February 1779, immediately prior to Beach's occupancy, it was described as a 'House Elegantly Furnish'd ... next the Bishop of Salisbury's ... Very Roomy and Convenient ... with excellent offices, situated within a sixpenny fare of the rooms, play-house and markets; to be lett immediately, ready furnished. A genteel private family, that would take care of the furniture, may have it on reasonable terms'.[45] Gainsborough's Abbey Street rooms were certainly wallpapered[46] and a number of his portraits from the early 1760s such as *Robert, Earl Nugent* (private collection) and *Matthew Hale* (Birmingham City Art Gallery) probably reflect the appearance of the painting room which was on the first floor, directly above the millinery. Gainsborough is said to have complained to Garrick that portraiture forced him to 'stew ... in an elegant carpeted damn'd dungeon'[47] and although the words may be apocryphal they do conjure up an image of the rather sumptuous surroundings in which the successful portrait painter operated.

Like Gainsborough, William Hoare lived 'in a handsome genteel manner' in Bath, at first probably on the east side of Queen Square and later in Edgar Buildings.[48] Neither he nor Gainsborough, Beach or Pine advertised in the local press, presumably because the practice was considered demeaning and these artists' picture rooms were prominently situated and marked with sign boards. In Bath, a relatively small city which could be traversed on foot or by sedan chair, the picture room display was probably more important than the production of prints or the use of press 'puffs' as a means of advertising. It is not known whether Gainsborough, Beach or Pine charged for entry to their rooms. Visitors to Hoare's rooms were certainly expected to part with money for the privilege, although it is not clear whether this passed to the artist or remained with the footman. The Rev John Penrose recorded 'Mr Brinsden put us to see Mr. Hoare's Paintings in Edgar-Row, and genteely gratified the Servant's Expectations, not suffering me to give'.[49] The minor portrait and historical painter Solomon Williams and the fruit painter and art dealer William Jones asked one shilling entrance, the same as it cost to visit the Society of Artists' exhibition in London.[50] Joseph Wright either charged or received handsome gratuities. In a letter from Bath on 30 April 1776 he outlined to his brother his plan to spend the summer painting a 'sea-piece, or some blacksmith's shop which will bring company to my rooms next season, for there is some advantage arising from their seeing only; there has been given at the doors £22 already, wch. more than pays a qrs. rent'.[51] It may be that only those portrait painters who also showed subject pictures or old masters were able to charge for entry. Gainsborough included old masters in his display and Beach owned Dutch and Italian paintings said to be by Rembrandt, Van Dyck and Guercino amongst others, although it is not known whether he exhibited these alongside his own work.[52] In London, after Gainsborough's death in 1788, his wife Margaret opened an exhibition of his remaining pictures at Schomberg House, charging half-a-crown admission, a fee she reduced to one shilling at the end of the first month. 700 visitors were recorded on the last day.[53] A flexible payment system was adopted at one exhibition in Bath in 1759. This was not strictly an art exhibition, but consisted of twelve life-sized waxworks of the King of Prussia and members of his court. Here sixpence was charged for servants and children, while ladies and gentlemen were left to give what they pleased, the expectation clearly being that they would give more than sixpence.[54] In 1781 Bateman sold season tickets for entry to an exhibition of stained glass and a device called 'Mr Storer's Royal Accurate Delineator' at Gyde's Assembly Rooms, but ran into difficulties when visitors attempted to transfer the 2s 6d tickets to their friends.[55]

Robert Edge Pine exhibited both historical compositions and portraits at Westgate Buildings in Bath[56] and it was no doubt in this city that he was convinced of the benefits of an elegant display room. An ambitious man of considerable ability but hampered by a 'morbidly irritable' temperament, Pine must have had Gainsborough's success in mind when he chose to settle in Bath in 1772.[57] Although he could not expect to rival Gainsborough during the two years both artists were in Bath, he probably picked up a number of commissions from those who could no longer afford Gainsborough's prices. When Philip Thicknesse fell out with Gainsborough over an unfinished portrait of himself he threatened to go and 'give Mr. Pine his fifty guineas'.[58] Pine probably learnt from Gainsborough above all others the commercial value of a good display room, and not long after leaving Bath he was to carry this message to America. In Philadelphia in 1786 Pine opened the first room in the United States specifically designed to exhibit works of art. The American painter Rembrandt Peale vividly recalled visiting Pine's house as a young man. 'When I entered Mr Pine's spacious saloon, I was astonished at its magnitude and the richness of the paintings which covered its walls ... and when I was with my father, admitted to his painting room, my surprise was increased on seeing a very small and slender man as the author of the great works I had just left'.[59]

A spacious and well-situated picture viewing room and a north-lit painting room were clearly the optimum requirements for the successful eighteenth-century portrait painter whether he worked in London, the provinces or overseas. When the artist James Northcote asked his brother to search for rooms for him in Plymouth he specified that they should be 'very good ones and one room which I am to paint in should have a north light or very nearly so'.[60] Gainsborough found in Bath two houses which satisfied the practical need for a good display room and a north-facing painting room, and his faith in property as an investment is borne out by the fact that during the second half of his 15-year stay he was spending in excess of £250 a year in rent, £100 more than he was to pay for Schomberg House on his move to London.[61] William Hoare also had a large north-south facing house in Edgar Buildings, George Street, and Joseph Wright's in Brock Street was equally well-placed. The houses in Westgate Buildings were not aligned north-south but had the benefit of carriage access from the Circus, proximity to the Hot and Cross Baths and cheaper rents. Westgate Buildings does seem to have been a favourite address for artists in the last two decades of the century. In addition to Beach and Pine a number of lesser-known painters including Solomon Williams (1757-1824), Elias Martin (1739-1818), Joseph Sheldon (fl.1781-1821) and John Sanders (1750-1825) all worked there. Thomas Robins the younger (1742-1806) moved into Pine's old premises in 1788.[62] Josiah Wedgwood's first Bath showroom was in Westgate Buildings.[63] More significantly a Mr John Cozens, almost certainly John Robert Cozens (1752-1799), Pine's nephew, had a house in the same street between summer 1779 and 1783, after Pine left for London.[64] Cozens may have exhibited Mediterranean landscapes in his picture room since he had only returned from Italy in April 1779. Although he was out of England again in November 1782 when the *Eidophusikon* was shown, De Loutherbourg's dramatic light and weather effects must have been close to Cozens' heart and it is just possible that he was in some way involved in bringing the exhibition to Bath.

In London, the first independent public art exhibitions of the 1760s enabled people to compare the work of one living artist with that of another for the first time. Bath saw the flowering of exhibitions arranged by individual artists in their own houses from the mid-century, but the town could not support anything along the lines of the London public exhibitions. In 1778 Thicknesse expressed the view that a public room in Bath should be allotted to artists where each could 'put up a Specimen of their Genius, we think that would be a fair Way, and the only fair Way of advertising the Public',[65] and in April of that year an attempt was made to inaugurate an annual open exhibition at Beach's house in Westgate Buildings. A 'puff' in the *Bath Chronicle* of 30 April expressed optimism:

A London Artist, who has seen the Bath Exhibition of Paintings, remarks, that (as it is only in its infancy) it reflects no small honour on the genius of the Bath artists in general. He observes, that several pieces by Messrs. Beach and Pine in particular, would be an ornament to a Royal Exhibition ...'

By 1778 however, Hoare was living the life of a gentleman, with few remaining artistic ambitions, Gainsborough had settled in London and Pine was nearing the end of his stay in Bath. It is no surprise that the scheme soon foundered. Despite this failure there is no doubt that between 1760 and 1780 the private picture rooms of Hoare, Gainsborough, Beach, Pine and Wright must have been an ornament to Bath and probably competed keenly with the other attractions on offer on dreary winter mornings. The situation and grandeur of Gainsborough's Abbey Street house, with its best parlour devoted to his paintings, must have set a standard to which other artists in Bath and beyond aspired. Recorded snippets of picture room conversation suggest that visitors were much entertained by the paintings they viewed, and spoke of portraits as if they were regarding the sitters themselves. William Dodd, as already noted, was admired for his 'lively eye' and a Gainsborough family group was proclaimed by one visitor 'the finest portrait she ever saw', and all the better for reminding her of an absent member of her own family.[66] Even the cynical Horace Walpole, who claimed to detest Bath, was so charmed by the magical atmosphere of Thomas Beach's rooms that he fancied the portraits living participants in the concert he attended there. Though few visitors may have shared the double pleasure of paintings and music together, many must have experienced, like Walpole, a sense of wonder at encountering faces they knew, as well as many more they would have liked to know, 'breathing in canvass' on artists' picture room walls.

Notes

1   D.M. Little and G.M. Kahrl eds., *The Letters of David Garrick* (Cambridge, Mass., 1963), Vol. III, p.1005, letter 907, to Hannah More, Bath 4 May 1775.
2   An undated typescript 'Index of Bath Artists' at the Victoria Art Gallery, Bath, compiled by Reginald W.M. Wright, former Curator at the Gallery, lists the majority of artists associated with the city. I have added a number of artists not recorded by Wright.
3   T. Bardwell, *The Practice of Painting and Perspective Made Easy* (1756), p.6.
4   Daniel Webb, *An Inquiry into the Beauties of Painting* (1760), p.35.

5   A. Rouquet, quoted by H. Belsey in 'A visit to the studios of Gainsborough and Hoare', *Burlington Magazine*, Vol. CXXIX (February 1987), pp.107-9.

6   Latterly Gainsborough and Hoare set aside more than one room for exhibition purposes. *ibid.*, pp.108-9.

7   *Bath Chronicle*, 14 September and 12 October 1786.

8   D. Foskett, *Miniatures, Dictionary and Guide* (Woodbridge, 1990), p.609; *Bath Chronicle, 5 April 1764.*

9   Charles Dack, *Sketch of the Life of Thomas Worlidge* (Peterborough, 1907), p.11.

10   D.E. Williams, *The Life and Correspondence of Sir Thomas Lawrence, Kt.* (1831), Vol. I, pp.86-7.

11   M. Woodall ed., *The Letters of Thomas Gainsborough* (1963), p.157, letter 87, to James Unwin, Bath 4 December 1763.

12   H. Walpole, *Anecdotes of Painting in England: 1760-1795*, F.W. Hilles and P.B. Daghlian eds. (New Haven and London, 1937), pp.20-2.

13   K.E. James, 'Concert Life in Eighteenth-century Bath', unpublished thesis, University of London (1987), Vol. V, p.1033.

14   The use of artificial light in display rooms may have been commonplace, see Marcia Pointon, *Hanging the Head* (New Haven and London, 1993), p.80.

15   *Bath Chronicle*, 21 April 1782.

16   Rudiger Joppien, *Philippe Jacques de Loutherbourg, R.A., 1740-1812*, (exhibition catalogue, Iveagh Bequest, Kenwood, 1973), catalogue number 87.

17   *Bath Chronicle*, 21 April 1803.

18   Philip Thicknesse, *New Prose Bath Guide for 1778* (1778), p.48.

19   Mrs Collins travelled the country taking 'profiles' in three minutes for a price of 2s.6d.

20   Woodall, *Letters*, p.73, letter 32, to David Garrick, Bath 22 June 1772

21   Wright was with Humphry in Florence in June and July 1775, see B. Nicholson, *Joseph Wright of Derby* (1968), Vol.I, p.11. Wright may also have been encouraged to Bath by Josiah Wedgwood who had opened showrooms there in 1772, see B. and H. Wedgwood,*The Wedgwood Circle 1730-1897* (1980), p.54.

22   Wright arrived in Bath on 4 November 1775 and 'Enter'd upon Mr Sproules House 9th Nov. 1775', see Nicholson, *Joseph Wright*, Vol. I, p.13, n.2. The house rented by Wright can be identified from the Bath Record Office (BRO), City Rate Book commencing 24 June 1775.

23   W. Bemrose, *The Life and Works of Joseph Wright A.R.A., commonly called "Wright of Derby"* (1885), p.45.

24   *Bath Chronicle*, 10 April 1777.

25   *Bath Chronicle*, 14 June 1781.

26   *Bath Chronicle*, 14 November 1782.

27   *Bath Chronicle*, 5 December 1782. The house taken by Pine would appear to be part of or all of Hetling House, now known as Abbey Church House.

28   Woodall, *Letters*, p.157, letter 87, to James Unwin, Bath 30 December 1763.

29   Susan Legouix Sloman, 'Gainsborough and the lodging-house way', in *Gainsborough's House Society Annual Report, 1991/2* (1992), pp.23-43.

30   Philip Thicknesse, *A Sketch of the Life and Paintings of Thomas Gainsborough* (1788), pp.15-6.

31   Thicknesse, *Guide*, p.49.

32   Giles Walkley, *Artists' Houses in London 1764-1914* (Aldershot, 1994), p.3;
        James Ayres, *The Artist's Craft, A History of Tools, Techniques and Materials*
        (1985), p.33; *Boddely's Bath Journal*, 5 April 1762.
33   *Bath Journal*, 22 April 1745.
34   The pediment stones, the only surviving relics of Gainsborough's Abbey
        Street house, are currently in store at the Roman Baths Museum, Bath.
35   *Number 1 Royal Crescent Bath, An illustrated guide and souvenir* (Bath, n.d.).
36   A. Cunningham, *The Lives of the Most Eminent British Painters, Sculptors
        and Architects* (1829-32), Vol. I, p.331.
37   G.W. Fulcher, *The Life of Thomas Gainsborough, R.A.* (1856), p.61.
38   Edward Edwards, *Anecdotes of Painters who have resided or been born in
        England* (1808), p.104.
39   Ephraim Hardcastle (W.H. Pyne), *Wine and Walnuts or, After Dinner Chit-Chat*
        (1823), Vol. II, pp.12-13 (note).
40   Walkley, *Artists' Houses*, pp.9-10.
41   See W. Ison, *The Georgian Buildings of Bath* (1948, revised ed. Bath, 1980),
        p.98, fig,24 for a first floor plan of Gainsborough's house at 17 Circus as it
        was originally arranged.
42   Woodall, *Letters*, p.55, letter 20, Bath 24 November 1773.
43   Marcia Pointon, 'Portrait-Painting as a Business Enterprise in London in
        the 1780s', *Art History*, Vol. 7, No. 2 (June 1984), p.197.
44   Pointon, *Hanging the Head*, p.44.
45   *Bath Chronicle*, 28 January, 4 February and 11 February 1779.
46   Sloman, 'Gainsborough and the lodging-house way', pp.26, 28.
47   Hardcastle, *Wine and Walnuts*, Vol. II, p.223.
48   G. Vertue, 'Note Books Volume III', *The Twenty-Second Volume of the Walpole
        Society 1933-34* (1934), p.149; BRO, transcripts of Walcot Church Rate Books
        from 1742-56 show Hoare's name consistently next or next but one to that
        of silversmith and toyman Paul Bertrand whose house is known to have
        been in Queen Square (*Bath Journal*, 10 November 1775).
49   Brigitte Mitchell and Hubert Penrose eds., *Letters from Bath 1766-1767 by
        the Rev. John Penrose* (Gloucester, 1983), p.192.
50   *Bath and Bristol Chronicle*, 19 October 1769 and 16 November 1786. See J. Ball,
        Paul and Thomas Sandby (Cheddar, 1985), pp.182-3 for the pricing system
        for London public exhibitions.
51   Bemrose, *Joseph Wright*, pp.45-6.
52   Belsey, 'A visit to the studios', p.108; *Bath Chronicle*, 21 April 1803.
53   Jack Lindsay, *Gainsborough, His Life and Art* (1981), p.199.
54   *Boddely's Bath Journal*, 24 December 1759.
55   *Bath Chronicle*, 31 May 1781.
56   Thicknesse, *Guide*, pp.48-9.
57   R.G. Stewart, *Robert Edge Pine, A British Portrait Painter in America 1784-1788*
        (Washington, 1979), p.23, and Edwards, *Anecdotes*, pp.172-3.
58   Thicknesse, *Sketch*, p.30.
59   Stewart, *Robert Edge Pine*, p.25.
60   Nigel Surry, 'James Northcote at Portsmouth', *Burlington Magazine*,
        Vol. CXXXVI, No. 1093 (April 1994), p.235, note 7.

61   Gainsborough's Abbey Street house cost him £150 per annum for the duration of his 14-year lease from 1760-1774. At the Circus he was probably paying in excess of £100 per annum fom 1767-1774. The wing of Schomberg House in London which he rented from 1774 cost £150 a year, see William T. Whitley, *Thomas Gainsborough* (1915), p.108.

62   *Bath Chronicle*, 22 October 1788.

63   See note 21 above.

64   BRO, City Rate Book commencing 24 June 1779, through to City Rate Book commencing 25 December 1782. See also K. Sloan, *Alexander and John Robert Cozens: the Poetry of Landscape* (New Haven and London, 1986), pp.136-7 and 99-103.

65   Thicknesse, *Guide*, p.49.

66   Sloman, 'Gainsborough and the lodging-house way', p.28.

RECORDED VISITS TO GAINSBOROUGH'S PICTURE ROOMS IN BATH

(a)   P.C. Yorke, *The Diary of John Baker* (1931), pp.251-2. On 3 December 1772 Baker visited Hoare and Gainsborough's rooms.

(b)   Lady Llanover ed., *The Autobiography and Correspondence of Mary Granville, Mrs Delany*, (1861), Vol. III, p.605. Mrs Delany's visit to Gainsborough's rooms was on 23 October 1760.

(c)   E. and F. Anson (eds.), *Mary Hamilton* (1925), p.26. Mary Hamilton visited Gainsborough's rooms in May 1774.

(d)   The Huntington Library, San Marino, California, MS Journal of Tours in England and France by Samuel Ireland of Norfolk Street, London, 1753-90, HM 31435, f.41. Ireland records he 'Call'd at Gainsborough'. The same day he attended the opening of the new Upper Assembly Rooms: this event identifies the date as 30 September 1771. (I am indebted to Hugh Belsey for this MS reference).

(e)   M. Elwyn, *The Noels and the Milbankes* (1967), p.37. In a letter of 24 February 1774 Elizabeth Noel recorded a visit to Hoare and Gainsborough's rooms.

(f)   William T. Whitley, *Thomas Gainsborough* (1915), p.107, refers to Eliza Orlebar's visit to Hoare and Gainsborough on 12 April 1774.

(g)   Brigitte Mitchell and Hubert Penrose eds., *Letters from Bath 1766-67 by the Rev. John Penrose* (Gloucester, 1983), p.40. Penrose records that his wife and daughter went 'to see the Pictures' on 18 April 1766. There follows a description of what appears to be Gainsborough's *The Byam Family* (now at Marlborough College). On 22 May 1766 the Penroses 'went to see Gainsborough's Portraits', *ibid.*, p.137.

(h)   Hugh Belsey, 'A visit to the studios of Gainsborough and Hoare', *Burlington Magazine*, Vol. CXXIX (February 1987), pp.107-9, publishes an account by Dorothy Richardson of her visit to Hoare and Gainsborough's rooms in May 1770.

Penrose and Mrs Delany's visits were to Gainsborough's Abbey Street address, all the other references are to 17 Circus.

Acknowledgements

I should like to thank Colin Johnston and Mary Blagdon of the Bath Record Office; Hugh Belsey of Gainsborough's House, Sudbury; Trevor Fawcett; my colleagues at the Victoria Art Gallery; and all the staff at the Yale Center for British Art at New Haven.

JEROM MURCH AND BATH POLITICS 1833-1879

Alex Kolaczkowski

Sir Jerom Murch, JP, DL was knighted belatedly in May 1894, the year before his death, in recognition of his achievements in Bath. The significance of his contribution to the political, legal, cultural, philanthropic and social life of the city led to the following observation in his funeral oration:

> The history of sixty years in this place is the history of his service. With uncooled ardour he battled again and again for instruction, for literature, for the prosperity of the people, for their recreation and their health. For righteous laws and expanding liberties he stood as champion.[1]

Apart from undertaking a prodigious number of non-political voluntary duties for the benefit of the city, for example in connection with the Mechanics' Institute/Athenaeum, the Bath Royal Literary and Scientific Institution, the Mineral Water Hospital, the Poor Law Board of Guardians, the Bath and West of England Society, the committee of the Royal Victoria Park, schools' governing bodies and the county and city judiciary, during the years 1833-79 he also became leader of Bath's Liberals and subsequently entered local government. He completed the first four of his seven mayoralties for the city, set a new agenda for municipal activism and in 1873, between bouts of mayoral service, he was persuaded to stand for one of the city's parliamentary seats. More than any other individual, Murch represented the new breed of civic reformer whose municipal mission characterized the last four decades of the nineteenth century.

In municipal politics Murch's name was a byword for courteous urbanity and he was renowned for his skills in negotiating every treacherous 'shoal and quicksand' of council committee meetings.[2] His broad range of interests and duties enabled him to operate within all the key elite structures of the city and form an unrivalled personal network of influence. However, this well-connected, scrupulous negotiator, the 'safeguard and antiseptic' of municipal life,[3] was no

1. Sir Jerom Murch: bronze bust by Sir Thomas Brock, RA, presented by the citizens of Bath to the corporation in 1895. (*Reproduced by courtesy of the Victoria Art Gallery, Bath & North East Somerset Council*)

moderate but held extreme political views, forged through his commitment to Unitarianism, that cerebral 'Frigid Zone' of Dissent.[4] During the 1830s and 40s in Bath, extreme Evangelicals, in particular members of the Trinitarian Bible Society who had quit the British and Foreign Bible Society parent group in protest at the continued presence of Unitarians, believed that to encounter Unitarian beliefs not only compromised the Lord's honour but threatened the eternal safety of their souls.[5]

Murch was born in Devonshire in 1807 and arrived in Bath in 1833 as the impecunious new pastor for the Trim Street Unitarian Chapel. His early campaigning activities, during which he became spokesman for the Dissenting community, laid the foundations of his civic career.[6] It was observed that to be a member of any of the denominations of 'Old Dissent', whether Baptist, Independent, Presbyterian or Quaker, was to be politicized as 'a radical of the first water and so far as the Church is concerned a revolutionist, yea a destructive'.[7] This was axiomatic purely on legal grounds because of their opposition to church rates which were removed only in 1868, and to the restrictions on higher education and burial, fully remedied only by 1871 and 1880 respectively. To be a Unitarian was to be on the margins of Dissent itself and to espouse an ultra-radical commitment to individual liberty. Apart from these generic politicizing factors, Bath was a bastion of Evangelicalism whose impassioned dogmatism was diametrically opposed to Murch's philosophy, and served to intensify religious conflicts which were of paramount importance at that time.[8] Also, the city was notably religious even at a time of religious obsession and scored a formidable 79.1 on Inglis's index of attendance, calculated from data collected in the religious census of 1851.[9]

A case of 'clergyman's throat' caused Murch to retire from the chapel by 1846, and an inheritance from his wife's family enabled and obliged him to become involved in municipal politics. In the spirit of the civic gospel which was to be articulated so powerfully from the Birmingham pulpits of the Reverends Dawson and Dale, and made a reality during the mayoralties of Joseph Chamberlain between 1873 and 1876, Murch recognized political service as part of his religious witness. In an age when those classes which regarded themselves as respectable identified closely with religion, as an ex-pastor bringing his sense of mission to his political duties he was the epitome of this *leitmotif* of the age: the identification of the secular with the sacred.

Bath was a centre of radicalism when Murch arrived in the 1830s. During the Chartist agitations for political reform Henry Vincent, the 'Young Demosthenes' of the movement, remarked after a meeting at the Guildhall, 'radicalism was never so honoured in any town or city in the nation'.[10] The Reform Act of 1832 had made Bath one of the most democratic boroughs in the country by enfranchising one in three adult males as opposed to the one in five typical for the average borough. Bath's new electorate had not only returned Major-General Palmer, a reforming Whig, but also John Arthur 'Tear 'em' Roebuck, the ultra-Radical and 'master of invective'.[11] Joseph Hume, the Radical MP, had recommended him to the city and

Roebuck was to collaborate with Hume and Francis Place as advisors to the London Working Men's Association when the Charter was devised.

Together, Roebuck and Palmer were described by their Tory opponents as representative only of the 'lanes and alleys of Bath'.[12] However, in the absence of any optimism concerning the outcome of the 1832 election, even the reactionary amongst the local Tories supported the third candidate, William Hobhouse, who was a traditional Whig. The reformers lost their seats to the Tories Viscount Powerscourt and William Ludlow Bruges in the 'Drunken Election' of 1837, but Roebuck and Lord Duncan, who had replaced Palmer as Radical candidate, regained them in 1841 against the tide of Peelite popularity, and caused Bath to be described as a 'hot bed of all that is wild, reckless and revolutionary in politics'.[13] Although Roebuck lost his seat in 1847 and the Conservatives gained their first majority on the council since municipal reform in 1835, the hegemony of radical reforming politics was re-established quickly and can be traced up to the disintegration of Liberalism in 1886.[14] The Conservative revival was confined to the years 1847-51, and by the 1860s the majority of the inhabitants were described as being 'arrayed in political fanaticism' and 'ultramontane republicanism'.[15] In the thirteen parliamentary elections between 1847 and 1880 there was always at least one Liberal MP and on six occasions the party held both seats.

Three phases of Murch's interaction with local politics will be examined, to provide evidence of his identification with the radical tradition of the city and to shed light on his influence and importance: firstly, his years as pastor; secondly, his civic and party activities of the 1860s; and finally, his involvement in the parliamentary elections of 1873-4. A critical consideration of the style and significance of his municipal improvement policies and the political changes which took place within the council necessarily lie outside the scope of this article.

Shortly after his arrival in the city the Reverend Murch cut his political teeth by speaking alongside local radicals like Mayor William Blair, Councillor William Hunt and Colonel William Napier – upper-class reformer, veteran and historian of the Peninsular War. For instance, early in 1836 Murch spoke at Todd's Riding School, a popular Radical venue, in support of state powers over the property of the Irish Church. Murch was the only clergyman on the platform and although overshadowed by Napier's rhetoric, his contribution was described as a 'bold declaration of war against tithe property'.[16] In open letters to the inhabitants of Bath he campaigned against the concept of an established church, the imposition of church rates, and the threat to discontinue the grant to the Roman Catholic seminary at Maynooth in Ireland.[17] Although Unitarians were at the opposing extreme of the religious spectrum from Roman Catholics, Murch's commitment to tolerance demanded that he champion their rights, which he did primarily by making public speeches on their behalf. He was also involved in petitioning parliament in support of Unitarian policies such as opposition to the education clauses in Graham's Factory Bill, which favoured Anglican instruction, and the campaign for the Dissenting Chapels Act. Although Unitarianism had been legal since blasphemy laws concerning the Holy Trinity were repealed in 1813, it was only the passage of the Dissenting Chapels Act in 1844 which affirmed their rights to endowments granted before the congregations abandoned orthodox Christology.[18]

Like other Unitarians, the most illustrious of which were James Martineau and William Johnson Fox, who has been cited as the most effective orator of the free trade movement,[19] Murch was a dedicated supporter of the Anti-Corn Law League. On 4 December 1845 he achieved something of a coup in being able to announce to Cobden and Bright, on the platform of Bath railway station, that Peel was to relinquish the Corn Laws. He was in charge of the reception of the campaigners, whom he described as 'illustrious and successful champions of a noble cause', and later spoke alongside them at a free trade rally in the city.[20] It was partly because of Roebuck's neglect of the Anti-Corn Law League that in the 1847 election campaign, which followed the repeal of the Corn Laws and the collapse of the Tory party, Murch decided to withdraw his support from this controversial representative. He also denounced Roebuck's 'ungovernable temper' and his lack of support for Palmerston and O'Connell, and concluded that he was unfit to serve.[21] Unitarian rectitude prevented Murch from identifying with the raw passion of such a political pugilist whose 'captious testiness' and 'peevish temper' were notorious.[22] Taking their cue from Murch, other Bath moderates repudiated Roebuck and although he believed that he had regained their support by the close of the selection meeting there is no collaborative evidence that Murch reversed his decision.

The 1847 campaign was unusually savage as Roebuck broke the habit of a lifetime and undertook personal canvassing which involved rousing nightly mobs on the streets. The 'ward meetings' were referred to by the hostile Conservative press as collections of the 'veriest scum of the city', the 'hooting and howling' causing 'annoyance and terror'.[23] Some Conservatives took umbrage because the mob appeared to be largely composed of non-voters and because cash from the Rothschild family financed the events. Also, some local Dissenters withdrew support from Roebuck as he had voted against Sabbath observance. To add to his difficulties, Roebuck had a formidable opponent in the person of Lord

Ashley, soon to become the Earl of Shaftesbury, who was a figure of national repute, commanded Whig support, and was leader of the Conservative Evangelical/Humanitarian reform lobby. He had led the movement for factory reform since 1832 and had been a prime mover in the struggle for the Mines Act of 1842. In Bath his campaign was supported by the arrival of delegates from the Manchester movement for 'short-time' work at a local meeting of the National Charter Association, and sufficient numbers of moderate voters were won over.

After his defeat, Roebuck claimed that he had been beaten, not by Tory superiority or even bribery, but by bigotry: the 'pitiful, shameful, wretched, miserable humbug' of the local Dissenters.[24] He declared on the hustings, 'I cannot forget the renegade Murch'.[25] Although ill health kept Murch from Bath at intervals immediately after the election, he was swift to reply to Roebuck's attack and observed: 'No risk of popular odium will ever deter me from doing what I conscientiously believe to be right'.[26] There was odium in plenty and a charge of dishonourable desertion, but despite this Murch was proved to be at one with the spirit of the times in his verdict on Roebuck. Radicalism had lost favour, Britain was poised to reject the Chartists' third and final charter, and was approaching that plateau of political complacency which distinguished the mid-century.

In accordance with Roebuck's warnings, the election of Ashley in tandem with Duncan presaged a Tory majority on the council the following November, and an end of the Radical mayors who had monopolized the role for all but one of the years since municipal reform. However, it was a fleeting victory. By 1852 the radical Liberals had regained a majority and there were no more Conservative mayors until 1869, and then only by invitation from the Liberal majority. In terms of the parliamentary seats, Ashley succeeded his father as the Earl of Shaftesbury in 1851 and his replacement was George T. Scobell, a Liberal landowner. When Duncan deserted in 1852, his replacement was the Liberal Thomas Phinn, son of a reforming Bath councillor of the pre-1835 civic regime. After acceptance of a minor government post in 1855, Phinn was in turn replaced by the Liberal William Tite who held the seat until his death in 1873.

The second stage of Murch's political career was characterized by the circumstances of his introduction to council in 1862. By this time he was regarded by all parties as the archetypal, contemporary version of the eighteenth-century master of ceremonies: an *arbiter elegantiarum* for the age of progress. He had become a monied member of the local gentry with numerous business interests, and such was his local prestige that he was invited to become mayor even before he stood for a seat on the council.

This was offered in order that he might orchestrate proceedings at the annual meeting of the British Association for the Advancement of Science, which was to be held in the city for the first time in 1864. The meeting was a success, attracting the third largest attendance in the history of the Association, and Murch was dubbed the 'type' or 'model' mayor at the conclusion of the event.[27] But he was not happy to interpret his role purely as ceremonial facilitator, and during the remainder of his first mayoralty he formulated a comprehensive reform programme for the city which incorporated: street improvements; the demolition of the ruinous *White Hart* coaching inn and the building of a modern municipal hotel with a new suite of treatment baths; an extension of the water supply; a solution for drainage and river pollution problems; and, to reinforce a clause of the 1851 Bath Act, the removal of the freemen's privileges and the instigation of public control of the commons. A comprehensive improvement bill was devised to empower the council for the regeneration of the city.

In 1865, during the planning of the improvements, an election was called and the second Liberal candidate withdrew at short notice. Murch was requested to stand and challenge the Conservative, Lieut-Colonel Sir James Hogg, who would win by default if no challenger emerged. The Liberals were determined to contest the second seat as the Conservative Arthur Way had won it in 1859, and they were anxious to re-establish the Liberal monopoly exercised in 1852, 1855 and 1857. The opposition had been boosted in 1857 after Way's first defeat by the formation of the Conservative Registration Society, which provided a potent challenge to the powerful Bath Liberal Association, reformed in 1847 after the defeat of Roebuck. However, Mayor Murch refused to accept the invitation as he was embroiled in municipal reform and therefore committed to neutrality. This played a part in Murch's temporary unpopularity and the short-term failure of his municipal programe, despite his publication of a pamphlet outlining part of his scheme in an effort to convert the public.[28]

The programme failed for a variety of reasons which included its novel scope, escalating costs, the unpopularity of recent activities of the council, and the attitudes of working men in the years immediately before the passing of the 1867 Reform Act, who resented the imposition of improvement programmes by civic grandees like Murch who in common with the Liberal leaders at Westminster seemed to be ignoring their political needs. In addition to local obstacles, there was opposition from central government because of the novelty of the speculative aspects of the hotel plan. In this, Bath was ahead of its time, for by the turn of the century municipalization had overtaken operations as diverse as theatre management, rabbit breeding and oyster production. As was observed in *The Times* in 1902: 'there is nothing too homely and nothing too enterprising for a local government body of the progressive type to take under its charge'.[29]

By the time of the general election of 1868 male urban householders had secured the vote; the majority welcomed further reform; and Murch was freed from the restraints of his civic position to re-emerge as Liberal partizan. Tite's personal prestige was such that his election was secure, so Murch assisted the second candidate, a Dr Donald Dalrymple from Norwich. As a Gladstonian, Dalrymple appealed to the radical roots of the Bath electorate, augmented by over 1,700 new voters, which healed the rift between erstwhile Chartists and their heirs who had joined the new Bath Working Men's Reform Association, and the middle-class Liberal Association. Despite this accord, the excesses of the formidable Liberal mob dominated the 1868 election campaign. For example, a riot occurred in the Guildhall when Sir James Hogg attempted to hold a meeting. A cacophany of farmyard noises made it impossible for his speech to be heard and the people's spokesman, Councillor Richard Edwards, was first 'tossed like a shuttlecock', then propelled towards the stage from the shoulders of the crowd.[30] This signalled a general brawl that police seemed unable, and according to Conservative opinion, unwilling to prevent.

Murch, the 'Radical Oracle', refused to condemn his followers for the affray, blamed Conservative provocation, and aggravated his opponents further by staging a torch-lit Liberal procession enlivened by 'Chinese lanthorns' and a band, whilst his opponents were limited to offering free private dinners out of reach of the populace. Murch was criticised for 'conduct unworthy of a gentleman or magistrate' and was accused of operating a closed borough of 'concentrated rottenness' from his library.[31] The result of the turbulent campaign was a double Liberal victory, buoyed up by the national mood of support for Gladstone and the anticipation of brisk reform.

The city experienced an unusual run of four elections between May 1873 and February 1874, which form a third significant phase in shaping and limiting Murch's career as local politician. In the words of George Goschen MP, Bath became a 'great electoral battlefield'[32] on which Murch appeared as a candidate and then as a party worker helping to secure a Liberal victory. By 1872 Gladstone's first ministry was at the 'exhausted volcano' stage in the image so aptly invoked by Disraeli,[33] as the major reform programme petered out and public irritation over incidents such as the Alabama arbitration reached a crescendo in response to the unpopular Licensing Act of 1872. Dalrymple's support for this and his championship of a rehabilitation bill for habitual drunkards alienated those who objected to controls on drinking and those who disliked the threat of increased taxes. His dismissal of a scheme for permissive legislation which sought local licensing regulations also sacrificed the support of local temperance men. Passions were so inflamed that the absence of the popular William Tite caused the annual public address from the members to be abandoned and Dalrymple had a closed session for ticket-holding supporters, as Hogg had been obliged to do in 1868.

Despite the national unpopularity of Liberalism and therefore the importance of maintaining municipal control, Murch refused the mayoralty in 1872 and promoted the election of a Conservative, Robert Stickney Blaine, who had settled in Bath in the late 1860s after amassing a fortune as a colonial merchant. He had purchased 'Summerhill' close to Murch's home on the slopes of Lansdown, replaced the late John Shum as councillor in the spring of 1872, and was later to become the leader of the local Conservatives. He became a member of both the Bath Royal Literary and Scientific Institution and the Mineral Water Hospital committees by 1874 and the Bath and County Club committee by 1875 when he also became a JP. In 1886, when the Liberal vote fragmented, he became MP for the city. Murch encouraged Blaine to take office as he believed this would not damage the Liberal cause, and it would be advantageous for members of Bath's economic elite of the upper-town to involve themselves in civic affairs.

However, this non-party initiative was eclipsed by the elections which started in May 1873 after the death of William Tite. Murch was prevailed upon to stand but his support for disestablishment and all aspects of Gladstonianism, apart from the generally popular Education Act of 1870, rendered him unlikely to succeed. He was local chairman of the Birmingham National Education League, a body pledged to remove the vexed Clause 25 of the Education Act which permitted the financial support of poor children at denominational schools. Ideally, the campaigners aimed to remove the Act in its entirety and replace the School Board plan of filling gaps left by denominational provision with a purely secular system. Also, Murch was supported in his campaign by individuals who were reviled in elite Conservative circles, for example the ultra-Radical Councillor Richard Edwards, the cheese-factor; Councillor James Clark, the solicitor; and also Handel Cossham, the Bristol-based temperance campaigner and colliery owner who had been involved in a recent scandal concerning misappropriation of funds. Cossham was described by the Conservative press as a 'hack demagogue ... virulent assailant of the Church' and Murch's political 'godfather'.[34]

ELECTORS OF BATH.

Two Candidates are each soliciting from you the highest honours you can confer upon them. Let us then examine well the claims of each, so that we may "render honour to whom honour is due."

I respectfully invite you then, to

Look on this Picture.

Mr. MURCH is an old and highly-esteemed Citizen of Bath, and has long identified himself with all its social and public life.

Mr. MURCH is a man of whom Bath may well be proud for his many literary attainments.

Mr. MURCH, as your Representative in Parliament, has the matured wisdom acquired by a large and varied experience of more than forty years of an active public life.

Mr. MURCH, by his zeal and munificence in the restoration of our noble and beautiful Abbey, has proved that his Christian charity is higher and greater than his sectarianism.

Mr. MURCH has either initiated and liberally supported, or both, many public movements in Bath, all tending to increase its interest or renown.

Mr. MURCH has, for a long series of years, not only been a liberal subscriber to, but an active worker for, all our great Public Benevolent Institutions.

Mr. MURCH, from his long useful and active life amongst us, knows our wants, and can therefore truly represent our varied interests.

And on this.

Lord CHELSEA is a recent importation amongst us—is simply a political partizan, and— **Nothing more.**

Lord CHELSEA (if report speaks truly) has his political speeches made for him. These he has to learn, repeat, and— **Nothing more.**

Lord CHELSEA, as your Representative in Parliament has all his experience to acquire. He has only the "Shibboleth" of his party. This he can pronounce, and— **Nothing more.**

Lord CHELSEA is a Churchman, and— **Nothing more.**

Lord CHELSEA can only *promise* to do this, and— **Nothing more.**

Lord CHELSEA, if elected, (?) *may* do this, and— **Nothing more.**

Lord CHELSEA, ignorant of these, can represent *his party only.* This, and— **Nothing more.**

Fellow Electors, can you then for a moment doubt which to choose? If you will, you can now *do yourselves the honour of being represented* by one of *yourselves,* by one who has lived and moved amongst us all his life ; whom, therefore we *thoroughly know,* and can therefore *thoroughly trust.*

Hesitate then not for an instant between one who is only a Titled Lord, and—**Nothing more,** and one whose life-long work has been to realize amongst us the Poet's idea of "The noblest work of God."

AN ELECTOR.

C. T. CULLIFORD. PRINTER, PARSONAGE LANE, WESTGATE STREET, BATH.

2. Liberal election poster , 1873. (*Reproduced by courtesy of Bath Record Office*)

ELECTORS OF BATH!

VOTE AGAINST JEROM MURCH:
The supporter of a Ministry who deprived Bath of its Free Grammar School, and are destroying other similar Institutions endowed by the piety and beneficence of our Forefathers.

VOTE AGAINST JEROM MURCH:
The supporter of a Ministry who turned out the Woolwich Dock Yard Men to starve.

VOTE AGAINST JEROM MURCH:
The supporter of a Ministry who sought to deprive the toiling working classes of the east end of London of the use and enjoyment of the people's Forest at Epping.

VOTE AGAINST JEROM MURCH:
The supporter of a Ministry who involved us in the muddle and disgrace of the Alabama Arbitration, with the consequent penalty of £3,000,000 to £4,000,000.

VOTE AGAINST JEROM MURCH:
The supporter of a Ministry who opposed Professor Fawcett's Bill, for extending the benefits of Trinity College, Dublin, and were beaten.

VOTE AGAINST JEROM MURCH:
Who supports the Birmingham League in attempting to deprive the poor of the most valuable portion of the Education Act, viz. : the Religious Denominational Teaching.

VOTE AGAINST JEROM MURCH:
Who helped to turn out Roebuck from Bath.

VOTE AGAINST JEROM MURCH:
Who, if Mayor this year, would have required £300 additional salary from the Borough Rates, a sum saved by the appointment of a Conservative Mayor.

VOTE AGAINST JEROM MURCH:
Who, as a Unitarian, cannot but be in favour of the disestablishment of the Church.

VOTE THEREFORE AGAINST JEROM MURCH:
As, surely, it is too much that Bath should be MISREPRESENTED by a NORWICH DOCTOR AND A UNITARIAN.

ELECTORS!
VOTE FOR LORD CHELSEA!

Who, by his age and energy, by his talent, by his industry, by his straightforward independence, by his refusal to trim, either on the Permissive Bill or any other question, and by his Constitutional and at the same time really Liberal Politics, shows his fitness to take a position of high standing in the House of Parliament, and will be such a Representative as Bath may be proud of, who has always opposed and will oppose the Income Tax.

3. Extract from a Conservative election poster, 1873. (*Courtesy of Bath Record Office*)

Murch's candidacy was an early victim in the 'torrent of gin and beer' of which Gladstone complained in 1874 at the collapse of his first ministry.[35] Murch's successful opponent Viscount Chelsea, followed the traditional Conservative line of supporting both the opposition of the licensed victuallers to restrictions on the sale of alcohol and also Forster's Education Act, and was thus neatly representative of liberty on the one hand and moderation on the other. Murch's adherence to the policies of an unpopular government, his political extremism and his Unitarianism, which still alienated the Evangelical majority, eroded his chances of success. He contested the seat at the nadir of Liberal fortunes when Bath already had a second unpopular Liberal MP, and at a time when his personal credentials were unappealing to voters. Liberalism was unpopular for its censorious attitude towards the drinking habits of the working classes and its libertarian reform policies. A hostile local correspondent later summed up Liberal campaigns as offering 'free church, free school, free land, free labour ... free love and free quarters to follow'.[36]

Murch's localist platform, developed as part of his municipal strategy, was inappropriate for Bath's conception of parliamentary politics. Black graffiti daubed on walls by his supporters claimed 'Bath needs no stranger' and 'Murch the man for Bath'; sentiments tellingly countered by the slogan 'Chelsea the man for parliament'.[37] It was cogently argued by one of Murch's supporters that Bath should not seek a representative 'whose interest in Bath begins and ends with his carpet bag in the York House',[38] though this was not qualified by an explanation of earlier support for Lord Duncan. Interestingly, the bruising contest did not destroy Murch's local credit for when the Liberals presented him with a commemorative *épergne* to thank him for his parliamentary efforts and his continuing public services, some leading Conservatives were annoyed to be excluded from the subscription list. As Murch was the personification of high culture and the civic ideal, their absence from the award ceremony was deemed a slur on their intellectual sensibility and municipal loyalty.

Chelsea's victory was popularly attributed to the support of the Conservative working man, and certainly Conservative election expenses were double those of the Liberals, and may have fuelled and refreshed the working-class protest vote. However, he represented Bath for only five weeks before the death of his father elevated him to the upper house as the 5th Earl of Cadogan and another election was required. Captain Arthur Hayter, a churchman, squire and son of the Liberal whip Sir William Hayter, had equivocal views, referred to by Handel Cossham as 'milk and water policy with the milk taken out',[39] and because of them was chosen by the Liberals to placate opposition. Ironically, polling at the June election was dominated by a power struggle within the Liberal camp. This was caused by a member of the National Education League, J. Charles Cox, standing in opposition to Hayter because of the latter's studious avoidance of a public endorsement of the views of the League on secular education.

Bath's Liberal mob resented this attempt to split the ranks and Cox's entourage was attacked on arriving at the Guildhall for a rally. The incident, summarized floridly in the Conservative press as 'Calumny, cajolery and cayenne!',[40] brought unwelcome national attention to the city. After a failed attempt to throw Cox out of the window, a group described as well-dressed tradesmen, wearing Liberal colours and blowing penny whistles, had showered the group with snuff and cayenne pepper which temporarily blinded Cox and injured both his agent and Francis Adams, Secretary of the Education League. Hayter promptly switched his allegiance to the League and Cox withdrew from the election, his original objective attained. After the incident, Hayter and Murch were reported to have rallied the crowds from a carriage, with Murch orchestrating the cheering as 'fugleman'. Joseph Chamberlain interpreted the incident as the start of a Nonconformist revolt which would be repeated at other elections as a warning to recalcitrant Liberals, but action was limited and that at Bath was the most significant gesture. The incident caused a question to be raised in parliament by George Dixon, MP for Birmingham and ally of Chamberlain. Henry Bruce, as Secretary of State for the Home Department, communicated with Bath on the subject, and Bath Council had a special meeting to consider the 'dastardly outrage' but no arrests were made.[41]

The weak Liberal cause was damaged further by this scandal which provided rich pickings for the opposition. For example, a contemporary squib billed Hayter to perform 'If at first you don't succeed' and speak on the subject of the 'shameful adulteration of Pepper and Snuff'; Murch was to offer 'Overboard he went'; and Mrs Hayter 'When I go bobbing around' accompanied by a juvenile chorus from Avon Street (a notorious slum area); with Richard Edwards on the tin whistle and the Express Band featuring 'Vagabond' Cossham.[42] Mrs Hayter's 'bobbing around' referred to a persistent canvassing campaign undertaken in the poorest streets of the city. Described as 'zealous and imprudent' by the Conservative press,[43] her activities were later claimed at a woman's suffrage rally to have played a significant role in the furthering of Hayter's campaign, and they endeared her to working-class Liberals who presented her with a gold necklace and diamond pendant as a token of their esteem.[44]

However, it appeared that the composition of Hayter's party or 'Happy Family' was, as suggested in the press, 'made up of creatures whose natural instinct is to bite and devour each other'.[45] The result of the election was a victory for Lord Grey de Wilton although the Conservative majority was reduced. In response the Liberals decided to reintroduce noble stock in the shape of Lord John Hervey, nephew of the Bishop of Bath and Wells and brother of the Marquis of Bristol, who was chosen to partner Hayter at the next general election. Before this, an early by-election was caused by Dalrymple's death in September and Hayter won his seat the following month. He was also returned at the head of the poll in the general election of February 1874. In response to the growing popularity of Disraelian Conservatism and, according to Liberal propagandists, 'the mere dangling of his filthy lucre',[46] Major Nathaniel Bousfield, the new Conservative candidate, took the second seat. Interestingly, Bousfield's 'lucre' had been generated by his family's cotton interests in Lancashire which made him an unusual nominee amongst the landowners and legal men who usually represented Conservatism in the city. His career was short, as effective local campaigning in which Murch took a leading role, coupled with the national swing back to Liberalism, caused the next general election of April 1880 to result in the return of two Liberal MPs for the brief period of Liberal unity which remained. Captain Hayter was partnered by Edmund Wodehouse, whose penchant for imperialism led him to join the Unionists when the Liberal party was wrecked on the reefs of Home Rule.

Murch continued to support Gladstonianism after his electoral defeat, and within the council chamber betrayed a partizan zeal which offended even staunch Liberals. In 1874 he engineered the election of an inexperienced Liberal protégé to the mayoralty, despite the fact that a Conservative candidate with sixteen years' experience of local govern-ment was willing to stand. To signal displeasure, the Liberal Councillor Dr Richard Gore seconded the Conservative nomination and attacked Murch's manoeuvre as being excessively partial and injudicious. Murch's nominee, Admiral James Aylmer Paynter, was a bluff naval commander whose declaration 'I'm for clean streets, Liberal principles and turning out Tories'[47] negated any neutral appeal generated by his social standing. It was stated in the Conservative press that the candidate was contemptible, and that 'political like all other scum will rise to the top'.[48] However, through his efforts on behalf of the city, Paynter became a popular mayor with all parties by the end of his two-year stint. Murch was elected to the next two mayoralties and after him the radical grocer

James Chaffin sat for three consecutive terms. Within local government Liberal hegemony appeared unassailable in the late 1870s, despite the parliamentary reversals. An average of thirty-five Liberals were returned in the council of fifty-six and all but two of the aldermen were Liberals, these two having been voted in as an unusual gesture of Liberal goodwill. Thomas Washbourne Gibbs, who became a Conservative alderman in March 1875, commented that under normal circumstances he was as likely to be chosen alderman in Bath as was the 'Grand Llama of Tibet' (sic).[49] Protests at the 'un-English and unfair ... exclusive dealing'[50] by the clique led by Murch and Thomas Jolly, his co-religionist and political ally, were common and it was observed that 'In no place in the kingdom ... is the spirit of Liberal partizanship narrower or more intolerant than in Bath'.[51]

In response to this criticism, it should be noted that Murch regarded the advancement of Liberalism as a sacred duty. He was loyal to Gladstone and Home Rule and opposed to imperialism, although his profound localism and enthusiasm for more statutory involvement in social improvement were more reminiscent of Chamberlain's brand of Radical-Liberalism. In 1878, at the conclusion of his fourth mayoralty, he was presented with a testimonial in recognition of his efforts for the city. Gifts included a marble bust of himself sculpted by Sir Thomas Brock, to be exhibited in the Bath Royal Literary and Scientific Institution, a Grecian-style silver salver and a bronze vase. In Murch's acceptance speech he observed that he had a liking for work but also felt a powerful moral obligation to labour for the public good, as for those with the leisure and aptitude it was 'hardly excusable to keep aloof from official life'.[52] This was representative of the *zeitgeist* of the age when municipal initiative became recognized as a major force in improvement politics. In Bath a gentleman who avoided civic service yet presumed to criticize the actions of the council was condemned by the outspoken Councillor Lewis as 'a mere slug, a worm'.[53]

It was observed at a banquet in Murch's honour in December 1864 that he had been instrumental in awakening a strong desire for improvement, and he saw himself as reviving the enterprise of his eighteenth-century predecessors on the council. It is apparent in retrospect that his work to capitalize on the assets of the city for the general good was not simply a revival of eighteenth-century-style municipal corporatism, but a mission reinforced with the moral armour of the nineteenth century which created a new form of social conscience and a determination to impose social improvement. Murch's vision for reform in Bath was partially realized by 1879. The Bath Act of 1870, subsequent Provisional Orders of 1875 and

4. Bathforum House: the original design for the Grand Pump Room Hotel by Wilson and Willcox, 1865. (*Reproduced by courtesy of Bath Reference Library*)

1876, and the continuing acquisition of private water companies, had improved water supplies. The Grand Pump Room Hotel, built on the site of the *White Hart* and functioning as a private concern with Murch as chairman of the board of directors, was regarded as one of the best provincial hotels.[54] The city operated the adjoining suite of baths and had gained total control of the hot spring outlets in the city by purchasing the Kingston Baths in 1878. Also, the Bath Act of 1879 extinguished the rights of the freemen, the remaining oligarchical structure within the civic administration. Although a solution for the drainage and flooding problems remained elusive, a new concept of municipal provision and service had begun to emerge which was to reach full efflorescence in the 1890s and the Edwardian period.

Murch's career in local government continued until his last illness in 1895. His definition of the duty of good citizens involved 'doing all the good they could on the widest possible basis and promoting the happiness of the greatest number',[55] which extended Benthamite utilitarianism by the suggestion of a broader altruism. His definition required concern for national politics and active municipal service, which mirrored Chamberlain's view of municipal duty as a noble and sacred obligation for the elite.[56] Although Murch and Chamberlain shared a Unitarian outlook and faith in democracy, and the same municipal idealism and rhetoric, Murch lacked the ruthlessness and industrially-based fortune of Chamberlain, and he failed to transfer to national politics after his initial disappointment. As Murch lost Bath in 1873, so Chamberlain lost Sheffield in 1874, but the latter's personal misery after the death of his second wife and parents in 1875, destroyed his religious faith and determined him to pursue politics on the national stage. Meanwhile the uxorious Murch, a dedicated localist and family man, remained content in Bath and continued his civic career which centred on furthering the cause of Liberalism and developing the scope of local government. His work was concluded fittingly with the successful completion of the new municipal buildings, a scheme devised and negotiated by himself, of whom it was said at the laying of the foundation stone in 1893: 'To no living person are the citizens of Bath more indebted than to yourself for the true development of her municipal institutions'.[57] Jerom Murch thus has a potent claim to be recognized as the most influential citizen and local politician in the city of Bath during most of the second half of the nineteenth century.

Notes

1   *The Inquirer*, 25 May 1895.
2   *Bath Chronicle (BC)*, 16 May 1895.
3   *Bath Herald (BH)*, 25 May 1895.
4   *Bath and Cheltenham Gazette (BCG)*, 12 January 1836.
5   Bath Library (BL), 'Proceedings of the Trinitarian Bible Society at Bath', Somerset Pamphlets, Vol. 6.
6   A. Kolaczkowski, 'Jerom Murch and Unitarianism in Bath 1833-45', *Transactions of the Unitarian Historical Society*, Vol. 21, No. 1 (1995), pp.15-29.
7   D. Fraser, *Urban Politics in Victorian England* (Leicester, 1976), p.270.
8   C. Smyth, *Simeon and Church Order* (Cambridge, 1940), p.203. This refers to the importance of Bath in the purchase of advowsons by the Simeon Trust; see also B. Stone, *Bath Millenium* (Bath, 1973), pp.90-1.
9   K. Inglis, 'Patterns of religious worship in 1851', *Journal of Ecclesiastical History* (April 1960), pp.74-86, especially p.80.
10   R.A. Challinor, *A Radical Lawyer in Victorian England. W.P. Roberts and the Struggle for Workers' Rights* (1990), p.12. For detail on Vincent, see M. Vincent, *The Vincent Printers* (New South Wales, 1980).
11   *BC*, 16 May 1895.
12   *BC*, 5 November 1835.
13   *BC*, 8 July 1841.
14   G. Davis, 'Image and reality in a Victorian provincial city: a working class area of Bath 1830-1900', unpublished PhD thesis, University of Bath (1981). This work moves beyond the contention that the upper-town of Bath and changing economy of the city extinguished radical politics, as argued by

R.S. Neale, 'Economic conditions and working class movements in the City of Bath, 1800-50', unpublished MA thesis, University of Bristol (1963). For an analysis of the composition of the council and strength of radical politics between 1835 and 1879, see A. Kolaczkowski, 'The politics of civic improvement: Bath 1835-79 with special reference to the career of Sir Jerom Murch', unpublished PhD thesis, University of Bath (1995).

15   *BC*, 18 May 1865, correspondence entitled 'Bath Redivivus'.
16   *BC*, 18 February 1836.
17   BL, *Bath Tracts*, Vol. 1.
18   J. Murch, *History of the Presbyterian and General Baptist Churches in the West of England* (1835). This publication was a significant piece of propaganda for the Unitarian cause. For another example of his efforts, see BL, J. Murch, 'Dissenting Chapels Bill – A letter', *Theological Pamphlets*, Vol. 1.
19   R. Cowherd, *The Politics of English Dissent* (New York, 1956), p.135.
20   BL, Sir Jerom Murch, *Scrapbooks Collection*, Vol. 1.
21   *BC*, 27 May 1847 and *Bath Journal (BJ)*, 29 May 1847.
22   *BCG*, 2 June 1847, quoting *The Times*.
23   *BCG*, 28 July 1847.
24   R. Leader, *The Life and Letters of the Rt. Hon. John Arthur Roebuck* (1897), p.187.
25   *BCG*, 4 August 1847.
26   *BH*, 31 July 1847; *BCG*, 4 August 1847.
27   *BC, The British Association for the Advancement of Science* (Bath, 1864), p.249.
28   BL, J. Murch, 'Reasons for Bathforum House with remarks on other municipal objects, 1865', *Bath Tracts*, Vol. 6.
29   *The Times*, 23 August 1902.
30   *BCG*, 19 August 1868; *BC*, 20 August 1868; Bath Record Office (BRO), Bath Council Minute Book, 5 September 1868, for reference to the damage caused.
31   *BC*, 29 October 1868; *BCG* 4 November 1868.
32   BC, 13 August 1874. Goschen was MP for the City of London and First Lord of the Admiralty, 1871-4. He was a friend of Arthur Hayter, the Liberal politician, and spoke at a rally at 'Cranwells', Murch's home.
33   M. Bentley, *Politics without Democracy 1815-1914* (1984), p.219, for reference to the importance of Disraeli's speech at Manchester in reforming the Conservative image. The specific reference was made at a speech in the Free Trade Hall, 3 April 1872.
34   *BC*, 1 May 1873. See also *BCG*, 5 June 1867; C. Press, *Liberal Leaders of Somerset* (1890), pp.25-35; *BC*, 11 May & 1 June 1907.
35   P. Magnus, *Gladstone: a Biography*, (1954, this edition 1968), p.228, quoting a letter from Gladstone to his brother, 6 February 1874.
36   *BC*, 29 October 1874.
37   *BC*, 1 May 1873.
38   *BC*, 8 May 1873.
39   *BC*, 3 July 1873.
40   *BC*, 3, 17 & 31 July 1873 for further details of the attack on Cox.
41   *Hansard Parliamentary Debates*, 93rd Series, Vol. 216 (HMSO, 1873), col.1553. See also BRO, Bath Council Minute Book, 5 August 1873.

42   BL, Poster Collection No. 62.
43   *BC*, 14 August 1873.
44   *BC*, 10 May 1877; *BC*, 28 August 1873.
45   *BC*, 3 July 1873.
46   *Bath Election News*, 29 January 1874.
47   *BC*, 29 October 1874.
48   *BC*, 5 November 1874.
49   *BC*, 11 March 1875.
50   BRO, Newscuttings Collection, 'Resignation of Edmund White – communication to the burgesses', 16 November 1874.
51   *BC*, 11 November 1880.
52   *BC*, 7 November 1878.
53   *BC*, 10 November 1870.
54   BL, 'Bath Redivivus, St Stephen's Review', 5 November 1887; *Bath Pamphlets – Page Collection*, Vol. 22.
55   *Bristol Mercury*, 26 November 1891.
56   C. Boyd ed., *Mr Chamberlain's Speeches* (1914), pp.41 & 73.
57   *BC*, 8 June 1893; *BJ*, 10 June 1893.

Acknowledgements

This article includes material from my research on civic improvement in Bath which was undertaken as part of a doctoral thesis. I would like to acknowledge the supervisory assistance given by Dr David Brooke and Professor Angus Buchanan of the University of Bath, and Dr Graham Davis of Bath College of Higher Education; the provision of archival and illustrative material by Mr Colin Johnston and Mrs Mary Blagdon at the Bath Record Office; Mrs Jane Carey's staff at Bath Library, in particular Mrs Elizabeth Bevan; and also Mrs Sue Sloman at the Victoria Art Gallery. I would also like to acknowledge Mr Trevor Fawcett of the History of Bath Research Group for his helpful observations.

174

INDEX TO *BATH HISTORY* VOLUMES I-VI BYAUTHOR

INDEX TO *BATH HISTORY* VOLUMES I-VI BY TITLE